Alarms & Excursions

Michael Frayn was born in 1933 in the suburbs of London. He began his career as a reporter on the *Guardian*, and became a columnist, first for the *Guardian*, then for the *Observer*. A selection of his columns, first published in four volumes, appeared as *The Original Michael Frayn*, and a collection of recent *Guardian* articles was published in 1995 under the title *Speak After the Beep*. He has written eight novels: *The Tin Men, The Russian Interpreter, Towards the End of the Morning, A Very Private Life, Sweet Dreams, The Trick of It, A Landing on the Sun* and *Now You Know*, together with a volume of philosophy, *Constructions*. He has also written screenplays for the cinema and TV: *Clockwise, First and Last* and *Remember Me?* as well as numerous stage plays including: *Alphabetical Order, Donkeys' Years, Clouds, Make and Break, Noises Off, Benefactors, Look Look, Here, Now You Know* and *Copenhagen*. He has translated Chekhov's last four plays, dramatised a selection of his one-act plays and short stories under the title of *The Sneeze* and adapted his first, untitled play, as *Wild Honey*. He has also translated one modern Russian play – Yuri Trifonov's *Exchange*.

by the same author

Novels

A Landing on the Sun
Now You Know
The Russian Interpreter
Sweet Dreams
The Tin Men
Towards the End of the Morning
The Trick of It
A Very Private Life

Plays

Alphabetical Order
Balmoral
Benefactors
Clockwise (*screenplay*)
Clouds
Copenhagen
Donkeys' Years
First and Last (*screenplay*)
Here
Jamie on a Flying Visit & Birthday
Look Look
Make and Break
Noises Off
Now You Know
The Two of Us
Wild Honey

Non-fiction

Constructions
The Original Michael Frayn
Speak After the Beep

Translations

The Cherry Orchard
Exchange
The Fruits of Enlightenment
Number One
The Seagull
The Sneeze
Three Sisters
Uncle Vanya
Wild Honey

Alarms & Excursions

more plays than one

Michael Frayn

Methuen

Published by Methuen

2 4 6 8 10 9 7 5 3

First published in the United Kingdom in 1998 by Methuen Drama,
215 Vauxhall Bridge Road, London SW1V 1EJ

Peribo Pty Ltd, 58 Beaumont Road, Mount Kuring-Gai
NSW 2080, Australia, ACN 002 273 761
(for Australia and New Zealand)

Methuen Publishing Limited Reg. No. 3543167

A CIP catalogue record for this book
is available from the British Library

ISBN 0 413 73280 0

Typeset by Deltatype Ltd, Birkenhead, Merseyside
Printed and bound in Great Britain by
Cox & Wyman Ltd, Reading, Berkshire

Caution

Alarms & Excursions

Alarms & Excursions was first performed at the Yvonne Arnaud Theatre, Guildford, on 15 July 1998. The cast was as follows:

Actor A	Nicky Henson
Actress B	Felicity Kendal
Actor C	Robert Bathurst
Actress D	Josie Lawrence

Directed by Michael Blakemore
Produced by Michael Codron and Lee Dean
Designed by Lez Brotherston
Lighting by Paul Pyant
Music by Terry Davies
Sound by John A. Leonard

Characters

Act One

Alarms:	Nicholas John Jocasta Nancy
Doubles:	Miles Melanie Laurence Lynn

Act Two

Leavings	Nicholas Nancy Jocasta John
Look Away Now	Aptly Bloss Charr Voice of Stewardess
Heart to Heart	Clifford Chairmian Peter
Glassnost	The Right Honourable the Baroness Armament KO GBH RSVP
Toasters	Spott Much Candle Voice of Speaker
Immobiles	Dietrich Chris Nikki Mother

The plays are to be performed by a team of two actors and two actresses:

Actor A and **Actress B**, both in their mid-forties
Actor C and **Actress D**, both in their mid-thirties

The likely distribution of parts would be:

Act One

	Actor A	Actress B	Actor C	Actress D
Alarms	John	Jocasta	Nicholas	Nancy
Doubles	Laurence	Lynn	Miles	Melanie

Act Two

	Actor A	Actress B	Actor C	Actress D
Leavings	John	Jocasta	Nicholas	Nancy
Look Away Now	Aptly	Charr	Bloss	Stewardess
Heart to Heart	Peter	–	Clifford	Charmian
Glassnost	Voice over PA	Lady Armament	–	–
Toasters	Speaker	Spott	Much	Candle
Immobiles	Chris	Mother	Dietrich	Nikki

Act One

Alarms

A table and four chairs. A phone, an answering machine. Three entrances: right, left and centre.

John, **Jocasta**, **Nicholas** *and* **Nancy**.

Nicholas Just us?

John Just you.

Jocasta Is that all right?

Nancy Wonderful.

Nicholas Perfect.

John We thought we'd simply flop down exhausted in our braces.

Jocasta Have a nice quiet evening together.

John Four old chums, grown bent and grey together over the years. Four weary fellow-travellers on the road of life, taking shelter for an hour or two from the night and storm.

Jocasta Something very simple in the oven.

Nancy Smells heavenly.

John The odd bottle of wine.

He fetches one.

Nicholas More and more like heaven.

Jocasta Just have a look at the oven . . .

She goes out right.

John Just open the wine . . .

He fetches an ingenious new corkscrew, and sets to work with it.

Then we can all . . .

Nicholas Flop down.

Nancy Exhausted.

John In our braces.

Nicholas Where?

John What?

Nicholas Where do you want us to flop down?

John Anywhere. On the floor. Under the sideboard. On a chair . . . On a chair! Why not?

Nicholas On a chair!

Nancy Brilliant.

Nicholas Any chair?

John Absolutely any chair that takes your fancy.

Nicholas The man's a prince.

Jocasta *enters right.*

Jocasta You found somewhere to park?

Nicholas Right outside.

Nancy For once!

John An augury, perhaps.

Nicholas This is going to be one of the great evenings.

John I'll just get the wine open . . .

He struggles with the corkscrew.

Then we'll simply sit and . . . I don't know . . .

Chink.

Jocasta Whatever one does when one gets the chance at last.

Nancy What *does* one do, as a matter of fact?

Nicholas So long since it happened.

Chink.

Jocasta Talk, perhaps?

Nancy Talk, yes! Talk, talk, talk!

Jocasta I remember talk.

Nicholas Get the wine open, possibly.

John Get the wine open, certainly.

He renews his efforts with the corkscrew.

Nicholas Or not even talk. Sit here in silence, why not?

Chink.

Nancy Relax. Be.

Nicholas Sip our wine.

John *withdraws his fingers sharply from the corkscrew.*

Nicholas New toy?

John The point is you don't have to do all that heaving and cursing. You just quite simply . . . No, hold on . . . Or possibly . . .

Nicholas Don't you put the . . . And then . . . ?

John I've got it, I've got it . . .

Nicholas No.

John Or . . .

Nicholas Try . . .

John Where are the instructions?

Jocasta I put them in the drawer.

John In the drawer?

Jocasta With all the other instructions.

Exit **Jocasta** *right.*

Nicholas Give it to me.

John It's all right.

Nicholas Let me have a go!

John No, if I can just . . .

Chink.

What?

Nicholas What?

John You made a little noise.

Nicholas No?

John It wasn't you?

Nicholas What sort of noise?

John Sort of . . . chink.

Chink.

There!

Nicholas I thought that was you.

John Me? Going chink?

Enter **Jocasta** *right, with the instructions.*

Jocasta The instructions for everything – in the drawer.

Nicholas Did you hear it?

Jocasta Did I hear what?

John Chink.

Jocasta Chink?

Nancy Chink.

Jocasta What do you mean, chink?

Chink.

Nancy There!

Jocasta What is it?

John That's what we want to know.

Nicholas Something in the house.

Nancy Some electronic thing.

Nicholas The phone.

John The phone? Phones don't go . . .

Chink.

Nicholas Listen!

John I've never heard a phone go chink!

Nancy But you've got this special system.

Nicholas This wonderful system.

Nancy That sends calls all over the house.

John Yes, but it doesn't go . . .

Chink.

It *is* you!

Nicholas It is *not* me!

John Something in your pocket.

Jocasta A pager, maybe.

Nicholas I haven't got a pager.

Nancy You've got your . . .

Nicholas What?

Nancy . . . little whatsit thing.

Nicholas What – this?

Nancy No . . .

Nicholas This?

John Pocketsful of the stuff.

Nancy That's electronic.

Nicholas Yes, but it doesn't go . . .

Chink.

Nancy What – me?

Jocasta Something in your bag.

Nancy Don't be silly.

Nicholas Let's have a look.

Nancy No!

Nicholas *I* got everything out of *my* pockets.

Nancy I don't keep things like that in my bag! There's nothing in there that could possibly go . . .

Chink.

Nicholas It's the opening thing.

John The opening thing?

Nicholas Your new bottle-opening thing.

John Going chink?

Nicholas To remind you.

John To do what?

Nicholas To open the wine.

Jocasta Yes. Come on.

Chink, chink.

Nicholas There! Twice! Chink chink! It's getting desperate!

Jocasta No, but as soon as you touched it!

Nancy Try not touching it!

Nicholas Put it down!

Nancy Listen . . . !

Nicholas Silence.

Nancy Wait . . . wait . . .

Nicholas You see?

Nancy If you don't touch it it doesn't go . . .

Chink.

Nicholas It's the oven.

Jocasta The oven?

Nancy You said you'd got something in the oven.

Jocasta The oven doesn't go . . .

Chink.

Nancy No, but the timer thing.

Jocasta The timer thing? The timer thing goes . . .

Buzz.

Excuse me . . .

She goes off right.

Nancy *Something* in the kitchen, though. The microwave.

Nicholas Or the food-processor.

Nancy The coffee-maker.

Nicholas The coffee-grinder.

The buzzing stops.

Nancy The toaster.

Jocasta The toaster?

John How can a toaster go . . . ?

Chink. Enter **Jocasta** *right.*

Jocasta Anyway, let's all just forget about it.

John But it's plainly trying to tell us something.

Jocasta But if we don't know what it is . . .

Nicholas It could be something important.

Jocasta It can't be *that* important!

John But it's plainly *meaningful*!

Silence.

Nancy Listen!

Nicholas What?

Nancy It's stopped.

Silence.

Jocasta Right. It's stopped. Where were we? What were talking about?

Nancy The chink.

Jocasta Before that.

Nicholas I can't remember.

Jocasta Open the wine, at least.

John I'm trying to.

Buzz.

Jocasta Sorry.

Jocasta *goes off right.*

Nancy Timer?

Jocasta (*off*) Sometimes you turn it off, and two minutes later . . .

Nicholas It's rather nice, the buzz.

Nancy Like bees.

John Soporific.

Nancy Summer afternoon.

Nicholas Glass of wine in front of you . . .

John Turn it *off*!

Jocasta (*off*) I'm trying to!

Buzzing stops. **Jocasta** *returns.*

Jocasta I keep meaning to get the man. Sorry.

Nicholas And at least we haven't got the . . .

Chink.

Nancy It's some sort of creature.

Nicholas Creature?

Nancy A cricket. A frog. Some sort of tropical frog. Perhaps it was someone's pet, and it escaped. Now it's trapped somewhere.

Chink.

It's getting desperate.

Chink.

It's in the ceiling . . .

They watch. Chink.

Jocasta It's the smoke alarm.

Nancy Oh my God.

Nicholas The house is on fire.

John Except it isn't.

Nancy Is it?

Nicholas The machine says it is!

John Well, it's wrong.

Nicholas A smoke alarm must know more about smoke than you do!

John It's lying.

Nicholas That's a terrible accusation.

John There is no smoke.

Nicholas There must be smoke.

John Look!

Nicholas I don't need to look. I can hear.

Nancy I can smell burning.

They all sniff. Buzz.

Nicholas I can smell buzzing.

Jocasta Sorry.

Exit **Jocasta** *right.*

Nicholas It's not a smoke alarm. It's an alarm alarm.

The buzzing stops.

Listen . . . You see? No buzz, no . . .

Chink.

Nancy Perhaps it needs a new battery.

Nicholas Perhaps we need the instructions.

Enter **Jocasta** *right carrying a drawer.*

Jocasta In here somewhere.

She dumps the contents on the table.

Nicholas These are all instructions? Instructions for gadgets? You have gadgets to fit all these instructions?

John Of course not. We throw out the gadgets when they break down.

Jocasta We never throw out the instructions.

John The instructions don't break down.

Nicholas Hair-curler . . . Eyebrow-trimmer . . . Toaster . . .

Jocasta We don't need instructions for the toaster!

She puts the book aside.

John We might.

He puts it back. Chink.

Nancy Perhaps it's trying to tell us it needs a new battery.

Nicholas Electric carving-knife . . . You haven't got an electric carving-knife!

Jocasta We threw the electric carving-knife out ten years ago!

She puts the book aside. **Nicholas** *puts it back.*

Nicholas You never know. Christmas Day. In rushes the man from across the street, desperate. Turkey on the table, fifteen people to dinner, and the carving-knife is going chink.

John Here we are – smoke alarm.

Jocasta Right at the bottom. The house could have burnt down by now.

Nancy I think it may just need . . .

Nicholas Yes, we heard you.

Nancy . . . a new battery.

Nicholas Don't be silly. Things don't go . . .

Chink.

. . . to tell you they need a new battery.

John *reads the instructions.*

John It needs a new battery.

Nicholas It needs a new battery. Obviously.

John Just help me . . . Thanks.

John *and* **Nicholas** *drag the table under the smoke alarm.* **John** *climbs on it.*

Jocasta Have we got a new battery?

Nicholas Of course you haven't. But if he takes out the old battery, at least it won't keep going . . .

Chink. Buzz. Exit **Jocasta** *right. Phone. Enter* **Jocasta** *right.*

Nicholas I'll get it . . .

Exit **Jocasta** *right.*

(*Into phone.*) Hello . . . ? No, he's dealing with the chink . . . The chink . . . Yes – he's standing on the table. Can he . . . ? No, OK, hold on . . . (*To* **John**.) Rather urgent.

Buzz stops.

John Cordless.

Nancy Where?

Enter **Jocasta** *right, holding cordless phone.*

Jocasta Here . . .

John Thanks.

Nicholas What do I do?

John Press nine.

Nicholas (*presses*) Nine.

Jocasta Not nine!

John Not nine!

Jocasta You're always doing this!

John I mean eight!

Jocasta Nine's the living-room! It's gone into the living-room now!

She starts to exit centre.

John You don't have to run after it! You can get it back, you can get it back!

Jocasta You can get it back if you can remember what to press to get it back, but you can never remember what to press!

Buzz.

Oh, no!

Nancy Living-room? I'll go, I'll go!

John Sit down, sit down!

Nicholas They didn't pay whatever it was for this wonderful system to have people go running all over the house like sheepdogs, rounding up stray calls.

John Just press . . . what is it?

Chink.

Jocasta You're going to make a mess of it, whatever you do.

Exit **Jocasta** *right.*

Nancy It'll just be quicker for me to . . .

Exit **Nancy** *centre.*

John Press Recall.

Nicholas (*presses*) Recall.

Enter **Jocasta** *right.*

Jocasta No! Not Recall!

John I mean Redial!

Nicholas (*presses*) Redial.

Jocasta Certainly not Redial! You'll never get it back now!

John It's that buzzer! I can't think with that buzzer going!

Chink. Enter **Nancy** *centre.*

Nancy It stopped just as I picked it up.

Jocasta It's ringing in the bedroom now.

Nancy Bedroom, right.

Jocasta It rings each extension in turn.

Nancy Which bedroom?

John Front.

Jocasta Back.

John Front first!

Jocasta Back first!

Exit **Nancy** *centre.*

John It doesn't matter . . .

Nicholas He sounded desperate.

John . . . because it'll end up on the answering machine. We'll hear it on the answering machine . . .

Chink.

(*To* **Jocasta**.) Buzzer, buzzer! (*To* **Nicholas**.) We'll pick it up on the answering machine.

Jocasta You can't pick it up on the answering machine! We're always trying to pick it up on the answering machine, and you can't!

John You can if you do it from the downstairs bathroom.

Jocasta No, from the study.

John The downstairs bathroom!

Jocasta The study!

Enter **Nancy** *centre.*

Nancy It wasn't the front bedroom . . .

Jocasta No, it was the back! *Now* it's the front!

John No, *now* it's the upstairs bathroom! (*To* **Jocasta**.) Will you stop that *buzzing*? It's driving me mad!

Nancy Upstairs bathroom?

Nicholas My turn.

Exit **Jocasta** *right.*

(*To* **Nancy**.) You open the wine.

Chink.

John (*to smoke alarm*) Oh, shut up!

Exit **Nicholas** *centre. Car alarm. Enter* **Nicholas** *centre.*

Nicholas Not yours?

John Or yours?

Nicholas Oh, *no*, not again!

Exit **Nicholas** *left.*

John (*to* **Nancy**) Open the wine. It sounds as if he might need a drink.

The buzzer stops. Enter **Jocasta** *right.*

Jocasta (*to* **Nancy**) What are you doing?

Nancy Opening the wine.

Jocasta Not with that thing!

John What do you mean, not with that thing!

Nancy I'm not very good with gadgets.

John It's *easier* with that thing!

Jocasta I'll get you an ordinary one.

Exit **Jocsata** *right. Doorbell.*

Nancy What's that?

John Doorbell.

Enter **Jocasta** *right.*

Jocasta Who on earth?

Nancy I'll go.

John *I'll* go! (*To* **Nancy**.) Wine, wine!

He gets down from the table and exits left.

Jocasta (*to* **Nancy**) Wait! Corkscrew!

Exit **Jocasta** *right.*

Voice on answering machine John, are you there or aren't you . . . ?

Enter **John** *left.*

John Oh, God, it's got on the answering machine!

Voice If I can't get hold of you I don't know what we're going to do.

John Give me a number! Get off the line! I'll call you back!

Voice John . . . ? I know you're there . . .

Enter **Jocasta** *right.*

Jocasta Who *is* this?

John I've no idea!

Voice You could end up in court.

Jocasta In court? What's happening?

John I don't know!

Voice It could cost you a lot of money . . . John . . . ?

Jocasta Pick it up, pick it up!

John Downstairs bathroom?

Exit **John** *centre.*

Jocasta (*calls after him*) Study! Study!

Doorbell.

Nancy The door . . .

Jocasta *I'll* go!

Buzzer.

You do the buzzer. No, leave it, leave it.

Nancy I'll do the wine.

Jocasta No! Wait! Don't do anything!

Exit **Jocasta** *left. Enter* **John** *centre.*

John I can't! It won't! Nothing happens!

Voice John . . . ? John . . . ? Will you please pick up the phone . . . !

John (*to answering machine*) I *have*! I've gone into the downstairs bathroom and picked it up, and it still doesn't work! (*To* **Nancy**.)

Not like that! You'll have your finger off!

Takes wine and gadget.

Voice John! Please!

Enter **Nicholas** *and* **Jocasta** *left.*

Nicholas Not mine.

John Oh, good.

Voice We're talking about several thousand pounds here . . .

John (*to answering machine*) Give me a *number*! Get off the *line*!

Nicholas What's all this?

John I have not the faintest notion!

Car alarm.

Oh, these bloody people and their car alarms . . . And that buzzer! I'll boot that buzzer into touch for a start!

Exit **John** *right.*

Jocasta I'll do it!

Exit **Jocasta** *right.*

Nicholas Blue Renault.

Enter **John** *right.*

John Blue Renault?

Nicholas Isn't that yours?

John Oh *no*!

Exit **John** *left, followed by* **Nicholas**.

Nicholas There's glass everywhere . . .

Enter **John** *left, followed by* **Nicholas**. *He hands the wine to* **Nancy**.

John Hold this. Don't try to do it.

Nicholas The stereo's gone . . .

Exit **John** *left, followed by* **Nicholas**.

Voice Several *hundred* thousand pounds . . . !

Enter **John** *left.*

John (*stops*) Several *hundred* . . . ? (*Calls.*) You did say *downstairs*? You did say *downstairs* bathroom?

Jocasta (*off*) What?

Nancy No, I think she said . . .

John Upstairs? She said upstairs? You pick it up from the *upstairs* bathroom?

Nancy Well, I think she said . . .

Exit **John** *centre.*

. . . the study.

Enter **Jocasta** *right.*

Jocasta The buzzer's completely jammed . . . ! What is it? What's he want?

Nancy He said was it the upstairs bathroom?

Jocasta Study! Study!

Nancy I'll tell him.

Jocasta *I'll* tell him.

The car alarm stops. Exit **Jocasta** *centre.*

Nancy I'll just open the . . .

Nancy *attempts to open the bottle, screams and drops it. Enter* **Jocasta** *centre.*

Jocasta What, what?

Nancy I'm so sorry. I think I've . . .

Jocasta Oh, no!

Enter **Nicholas** *left.*

Nicholas What in heaven's name . . . ?

Jocasta Her finger!

Nicholas You know you can't do anything mechanical!

Jocasta Is there an artery in your finger?

Nancy I'm fine, I'm fine.

Nicholas Hold it up in the air . . . You're getting blood over everything!

Jocasta Tourniquet . . .

Nicholas Tea cloth!

Nancy Don't fuss, I'm fine.

Nicholas No, but it's going everywhere! Newspaper! I'm so sorry about this.

Jocasta Casualty! Get her to casualty!

Nancy I just feel a bit faint . . .

Jocasta Casualty! Casualty!

Jocasta *and* **Nicholas** *hustle* **Nancy** *away left.*

Nicholas I'm so sorry.

Nancy I think I *did* get it open. I think it's pouring over the carpet.

Jocasta (*calls*) John! *John* . . . ! Leave that! Emergency!

Nicholas *I'll* tell him! You get her into the car!

Exit **Nicholas** *centre.*

Jocasta (*calls after him*) He's in the upstairs bathroom!

She rushes **Nancy** *off left.*

(*To* **Nancy**.) Keep calm! There's nothing to worry about!

Enter **John** *centre.*

John I *knew* you couldn't do it from the upstairs bathroom! Where are you . . . ? Where is everybody?

Voice Still here . . . Still waiting . . .

Enter **Jocasta** *and* **Nancy** *left.*

Jocasta Door-keys! Haven't got my door-keys!

John What in heaven's name . . . ?

Jocasta Bleeding! Bottle! Finger! Casualty!

John Oh, my God!

Jocasta Car! Get her into the car!

John *rushes* **Nancy** *off left.*

Jocasta Door-keys!

Exit **Jocasta** *right. Enter* **John** *and* **Nancy** *left.*

John Car! Broken glass!

Enter **Jocasta** *right.*

Jocasta Their car!

John Their car.

Exit **John** *and* **Nancy** *left.*

Jocasta What was I doing . . . ? Door-keys!

Exit **Jocasta** *right. Enter* **Nicholas** *centre.*

Nicholas Not in the upstairs bathroom . . . You didn't say the *study*? You didn't say the *attic* . . . ?

Exit **Nicholas** *centre. Enter* **John** *and* **Nancy** *left.*

John Door-keys! Haven't got the door-keys!

Nancy I think I'm going to faint.

John Car! Car! Get in the car!

Nancy *remains where she is, dazed. Enter* **Jocasta** *right.*

John Door-keys!

Jocasta Door-keys!

John On the hook!

Exit **John** *right.*

Jocasta (*after* **John**) Not on the hook!

Nancy I'm so sorry . . .

Jocasta (*to* **Nancy**) In the car! (*After* **John**.) I've just looked!

Exit **Jocasta** *right.*

Nancy I don't think I can quite . . .

She sits down and puts her head between her knees.

The buzzer stops. Enter **John** *right, with a large cast-iron saucepan.*

John (*after* **Jocasta**) Not on the hook!

Enter **Jocasta** *right.*

Jocasta I *said* – not on the . . .

She sees the saucepan.

John Table.

Jocasta Saucepan?

John Buzzer. Fixed the buzzer. Table!

Jocasta Table?

John (*searches*) Door-keys! On the table . . . ! Under the table! Move the table!

He puts the saucepan down on the table and struggles to drag it back into its original position, where it conceals **Nancy***, without noticing her.*

Doing the thing! With the door-keys! Put them down! Fell on the floor!

No sign of them there. Enter **Nicholas** *centre.*

Nicholas Not in the study.

John The door-keys?

Nicholas You.

John Me?

Nicholas Looking for you.

John I'm here.

Nicholas Slight problem with the . . .

John I know!

Nicholas Where is she?

John In the car!

Nicholas In the car?

Jocasta (*to* **Nicholas**) In the car!

Nicholas In the car . . .

Exit **Nicholas** *left.*

Jocasta Try the bedroom!

John The bedroom?

Exit **John** *centre. Enter* **Nicholas** *left.*

Nicholas The bedroom?

Jocasta (*calls after* **John**) By the bed! On the bed!

Nicholas On the *bed*?

Jocasta (*to* **John**) *Under* the bed!

Nicholas (*to* **John**) *Under* the bed?

Nicholas *goes towards the centre exit.*

Jocasta (*to* **Nicholas**) The keys! Her? In the car!

Nicholas In the car . . .

Exit **Nicholas** *left. Enter* **John** *centre, waving door-keys.*

John By the phone!

Jocasta In the car!

John In the car! Burglar alarm!

Jocasta Burglar alarm!

Exit **John** *and* **Jocasta** *left.*

Voice Three years, John – *five* years . . . !

Four pips, as burglar alarm is set, followed by warbling tone.

Enter **John** *left.*

John Five years?

Nicholas (*off*) She's not in the car!

Enter **Nicholas** *left.*

Nicholas Where is she?

Enter **Jocasta** *left.*

Jocasta She's in the car!

Nicholas She's not in the car!

John Five years!

Jocasta Alarm, alarm!

She bundles **John** *and* **Nicholas** *off left. Sound of front door slamming. Continuous tone from burglar alarm.*

Voice Come on! You can't just sit there with your head in the sand!

Nancy *sits up groggily from behind the table.*

Nancy Sorry. Just coming.

Jocasta (*off*) Keys! Keys! Who's got the keys?

John (*off*) I've got the keys!

Sound of front door opening. Continuous tone from burglar alarm turns to urgent interrupted warning tone. **Nancy** *subsides behind the table again. Enter* **Jocasta**, **Nicholas** *and* **John**, *left.*

Jocasta (*calls*) Nancy!

John (*calls*) Nancy!

Jocasta I thought she was in the car!

Nicholas I told you she wasn't in the car!

Jocasta (*calls*) Nancy!

John Alarm!

Jocasta Alarm . . .

Exit **Jocasta** *left. Four pips as burglar alarm is disarmed.*

John (*calls*) Nancy!

Exit **John** *right, searching.* **Nancy** *sits up again.*

Nancy Sorry. I can't quite . . .

She disappears behind the table again.

Nicholas What on earth . . . ?

Nicholas *drags the table out of the way. Enter* **Jocasta** *left.*

Jocasta Where on earth . . . ?

Nicholas Under the table!

Jocasta *and* **Nicholas** *rush* **Nancy** *off left. Four pips as burglar alarm is set, followed by warbling tone.*

Enter **John** *right.*

John She was under the table?

Jocasta (*off*) Lights!

John Lights . . .

Exit **John** *right to switch off the kitchen lights. Enter* **Nicholas** *left.*

Nicholas Lights . . .

He switches off lights by lefthand exit. Darkness. The slam of the front door. Continuous tone from burglar alarm.

Enter **John** *right, invisible in the darkness.*

John Stop! Wait! I'm still inside!

Crash as he runs into the displaced table. The continuous tone from the burglar alarm finishes. Silence. Chink. Groan.

Voice Come on, John, pull yourself together . . .

Doorbell. Knocker.

Jocasta (*off*) John, open the door! I haven't any keys!

Nicholas (*off*) The alarm's on!

Jocasta (*off*) Keep absolutely still!

Nicholas (*off*) Turn the alarm off!

Jocasta (*off*) Don't move, or the alarm will . . .

Another groan. Something moves in the darkness. A high intermittent warning sound from the alarm.

(*Off.*) I said, Don't move!

Nicholas (*off*) Turn it off! Turn it off!

Jocasta (*off*) You've got about fifteen seconds! Fourteen! Thirteen . . . !

A light comes on. **John** *is standing, with his hand on the switch and the saucepan on his head. The table is on its side.*

Nicholas (*off*) Come on, come on!

Jocasta (*off*) What are you doing?

Nicholas (*off*) Do something!

Jocasta (*off*) It's going to go off! It's going to go off!

Voice No? Sit down, then, and I'll tell you what this is all about.

John *takes the saucepan off his head and subsides, still stunned, into a chair.*

Now, listen carefully . . .

He listens carefully. Doorbell. Door-knocker. Hammering on door with fists. Flapping of letter-box. Buzzer. Car alarm. Police siren. The burglar alarm goes off.

Curtain.

Doubles

Two standard small hotel double bedrooms, arranged so that they are mirror images of each other. Upstage in each room is the door to the corridor. Beside the doors are boxed-off shower/toilets, back-to-back against the party wall. Double beds, also back to back against the party wall. The party wall itself is irregularly cut away as it comes downstage, as in a sectional drawing, so that at the downstage end it is entirely notional, apart from the back-to-back frames of full-length mirrors. Along the opposite wall of each bedroom is the same array of standard equipment: TV; a fitted wall unit that includes luggage stand, hanging space and built-in desk; a mini-bar; an electric kettle; a trouser-press. Downstage each room has a balcony.

LEFTHAND ROOM

Darkness. Then the lights come up as the upstage door opens to reveal **Miles**. *He is carrying an overnight bag and other travel impedimenta. He stops uneasily.*

Miles This room . . .

Melanie *enters behind him, also carrying bags and coats.*

Melanie (*anxiously*) Is it all right?

Miles (*eerily*) There's something familiar about it . . .

Melanie It looks all right.

He dumps his bag on the bed.

Miles TV . . . Mini-bar . . . Have we somehow . . . gone back in time to the hotel we stayed in last night? Look – it's the same balcony! It's the same view over the hotel car-park!

RIGHTHAND ROOM

Darkness.

Melanie (*matter-of-fact*) What about the bathroom?

She goes into it.

Miles Yes! The bathroom's different. Last night it was here.

He indicates the lefthand wall by the window.

Is it the hotel we stayed in the the night *before* last? Or have we . . . strayed *forward* in time to the hotel we're going to be staying in tomorrow night?

She comes out of the bathroom.

Melanie If it's *clean* – that's all I care about.

She starts to unpack.

Miles We must write to the Good Hotel Guide. 'One satisfied couple were specially struck by the charming sense of *déjà-vu* about the complimentary tea bags and sterilised milk.'

Melanie Aren't you going to unpack?

She lays out her stuff on the downstage side of the bed.

Miles Actually this particular pattern of cigarette burns on the carpet we *haven't* seen before.

He reads a notice on the wall.

'For the safekeeping of personal possessions the management is entirely irresponsible.' That's new.

Melanie I wish you wouldn't put your suitcase on the bed.

Miles 'Our esteemed guests are advised that chuckout time is noon.'

Melanie You could press your trousers.

Miles I could what?

Melanie There's a trouser-press.

Miles Good God, we haven't had a trouser-press before! I shall always think of this as the Place with the Trouser-press.

Melanie Sit down. Read a book, or something.

She comes downstage and inspects herself in the full-length mirror, indicated notionally by its frame, between the bed and the window, on the notional party wall . . .

Miles Read a book? All right.

He picks up the directory of hotel services.

'Why not relax over a pre-dinner cocktail in the intimate atmosphere of the Commodore's Cabin?'

Melanie To yourself.

She goes on inspecting herself, dissatisfied, in the mirror. He watches her, then turns back to the directory.

Miles 'As you sip you can study the choice of specially selected local and international dishes in our celebrated Downtowner Dining-room and Groll.'

Melanie At least take your suitcase off the bed.

He moves it on to the floor beside the TV.

Miles When you think of them all, though. All the people who've been in this room before us. Unpacked their bags.

He opens his bag.

Packed them up again. Dropped their lighted cigarettes on the carpet. 365 couples a year. They come through the door. They look round. She checks the bathroom. He reads out the funny English. Together they discover the complimentary trouser-press . . .

Melanie I'm going to have a shower.

She retires into the bathroom. He sinks down on the bed, suddenly gloomy.

Miles And then you think – how many rooms are there in the hotel? 200? 300? So every night 300 doors are opening, and 300 couples are coming in, and looking round, and reading out about the chuckout time and the Groll, and discovering the trouser-press . . . So that's 100,000 couples a year . . . 10,000 hotels, all the same. A thousand million couples. Every couple having the same experiences . . . All turning into the same couple, repeated a thousand million times . . .

He gives up his attempt at unpacking, overcome with gloom.

The lights come up as the upstage door opens to reveal **Laurence**. *He is carrying an overnight bag and other travel impedimenta. He looks round the room.*

Laurence Trouser-press.

He advances into the room, followed by **Lynn**, *also carrying bags and coats.*

Trouser-press, look.

Lynn So I see.

Laurence What?

Lynn Nothing.

Laurence Don't like it?

Lynn Lovely.

Laurence No different from the one last night.

Lynn Or the night before.

Laurence You liked them.

Lynn Did I?

Laurence It's only for one night.

Laurence Some sort of brown stuff spilt down the wall.

Laurence Well, that makes a change.

Lynn Very distinctive.

Laurence Come on! We'll be somewhere else tomorrow night.

Lynn I know. Somewhere like this.

Laurence Balcony. Nice view.

Lynn It's the hotel car-park.

Laurence It could be the gasworks.

Lynn You can keep an eye on the car.

Laurence Give it a rest.

Lynn That's all you worry about.

Laurence I know. Cup of tea?

Lynn No, thanks.

Laurence Kettle. All the doings.

Lynn I don't want one!

Laurence Mini-bar . . . You want a drink?

Lynn What's the bathroom like?

She looks into it. He goes on inspecting the equipment of the room.

Laurence Biscuits . . . biscuits . . . more biscuits . . .

Lynn *comes out of the bathroom.*

Lynn It's sanitised for our personal protection.

Laurence Good. No shortage of biscuits!

Lynn We've got our own biscuits.

Laurence Well, now we've got some spare ones.

He lays out his stuff on the upstage side of the bed.

I'll go this side, OK?

Lynn What are you asking for?

Laurence Go the other way round if you like. We're on holiday.

Lynn (*reads a notice on the wall*) 'Our esteemed guests are advised that chuckout time is noon.'

Laurence Noon? Right.

Lynn Chuckout time.

Laurence Aren't you going to unpack?

Lynn 'For the safekeeping of personal possessions the management is entirely irresponsible.'

Laurence Yes – don't go leaving your handbag in the room this time.

He unpacks. She picks up the directory of hotel services on the desk.

Lynn 'Why not relax over a pre-dinner cocktail in the intimate atmosphere of the Commodore's Cabin?'

Laurence Have a drink here if you want one.

Lynn 'As you sip you can study the choice of specially selected local and international dishes in our celebrated Downtowner Dining-room and Groll.'

Laurence Do you want a drink or don't you?

Lynn I want a nice grolled steak. Medium rear. With chaps and poos.

Laurence Don't go mad. You'll be up all night again.

He takes his trousers off.

Lynn What – pressing your trousers?

Laurence Why not? While we've got the chance?

He puts his trousers in the press. She watches him gloomily.

Lynn Funny, when you think there was someone else taking off his trousers in here last night.

She comes downstage and looks at herself in the notional full-length mirror on the party wall between the bed and the window.

Someone else in that mirror. Looking back at themselves.

Laurence Moaning away about everything.

Lynn Someone else the night before that. Someone else tomorrow night. Someone on the other side of the wall . . .

She sinks down on to the bed, overcome by melancholy. He inspects his bare legs.

Laurence Might as well have a crap, now I've got them off.

He goes into bathroom.

Miles (*calls*) Shall I come and scrub your back . . . ?

Lynn (*calls*) What?

Shall I come and work on various parts of you?

What are you mumbling about?

Melanie (*off*) What?

Laurence (*off*) What?

Miles I said . . . Oh, never mind.

He turns on the TV. The screen faces upstage, but there is the sound of an announcer reading a news bulletin in Rewindese, the language a recording makes when it's run backwards. He watches gloomily for a few moments, then presses the remote, and the news is replaced by the sounds of a Rewindese love scene.

Enter **Melanie**, *in a dressing-gown, from the bathroom.*

Melanie You're not going to leave your bag there?

He instantaneously switches back to the news. Pause. He becomes aware of her.

Miles What?

Pause.

Melanie What are you watching?

Miles No idea.

Melanie What's it about?

Miles Shortfall in self-adhesive envelope production.

Lynn I said . . . Oh, never mind.

She turns on the TV. The screen faces upstage, but there is the sound of an announcer reading a news bulletin in Rewindese, the language a recording makes when it's run backwards. She watches gloomily for a few moments, then presses the remote, and the news is replaced by the sounds of a Rewindese love scene.

Enter **Laurence**, *still trouserless, from the bathroom.*

Laurence Changed my mind.

She instantaneously switches back to the news. Pause. She becomes aware of him.

Lynn What?

Pause.

Laurence What's all this, then?

Lynn Search me.

Laurence Where's the whatsit?

Melanie Try the other channels.

She picks up the remote and presses the button. The sound of the love scene.

Oh dear.

She gazes at the screen, in spite of herself. So does he.

Miles She's trying to tell him she reversed the car into a bollard.

She switches off.

Miles Oh.

Melanie Somebody's going to fall over that bag.

Miles Me.

Melanie Probably. It was you last night.

Miles And the night before.

He puts his hand under her dressing-gown.

Melanie (*startled*) What?

He picks up the remote and presses the button. The sound of the love scene.

Oh dear oh dear.

He gazes at the screens in spite of himself. So does she.

Lynn She's trying to tell him something.

Laurence We don't want to watch this kind of thing, do we?

He switches off.

Lynn Oh.

She puts her hand on his bare knee.

Laurence (*baffled*) What?

Lynn Since you've got your trousers off already . . .

Miles Another letter to the Good Hotel Guide. 'One guest complained about the shocking flimsiness of his partner's underwear.'

Laurence They should be done by now.

Melanie (*pushes his hand away*) I've had my shower.

She begins to get dressed. He inspects himself gloomily in the full-length mirror, turning his head this way and that.

He goes to inspect the trouser-press. She inspects herself gloomily in the full-length mirror, turning her head this way and that.

Melanie Aren't you going to change?

Miles I have. Out of all recognition.

Lynn I don't look like that, do I?

I never used to look like that.

Melanie I thought we were going to eat?

Miles Do I exist as a continuous entity?

Melanie You know what'll happen . . .

Miles Close my eyes for a moment . . .

Laurence We eating, or what?

Lynn Do something to my face.

And when I open them . . .

(*In alarm.*) . . . I've vanished!

Melanie They'll have stopped serving.

Miles (*depressed*) No, I haven't.

He puts his face very close to the mirror, and contorts it as he examines it.

But is that really me?

Or is that some complete stranger gazing back at me?

She holds up a pair of trousers to examine.

Melanie Got a bit crumpled.

He glances round.

Miles Perfect.

He turns back to the mirror.

I suppose I'm talking to myself.

(*To his image.*) Hello!

What's it like in there?

She goes to fetch her handbag.

She returns and begins to make up her face in the mirror.

She puts her face very close to the mirror, and contorts it as she makes up.

Do *you* think I've changed?

I still look like me if I put a bit of make-up on, don't I?

He holds up the pressed trousers.

Laurence How about that?

She glances round.

Lynn Wonderful.

She turns back to the mirror.

I suppose I'm talking to myself. (*To her image.*) Hello!

How are *you* today?

You're trying to say something.

I didn't quite catch what you said.

You always speak at exactly the same time as I do!

She joins him at the mirror, to inspect the effect of her trousers.

Melanie What do you think?

Miles I said – perfect.

Melanie Not *too* creased?

Miles Wonderful.

Come here.

He indicates their image in the mirror.

That's us.

What do you think?

Melanie What do I think?

Did you say something?

What was that?

The trouble is . . .

You always speak at exactly the same time as I do!

He joins her at the mirror, to inspect the effect of his trousers.

Laurence All right?

Lynn I said – wonderful.

Laurence Not *too* creased?

Lynn Perfect.

Look.

She indicates their image in the mirror.

That's us.

Laurence I know.

Lynn Are we . . . all right?

Laurence Are we all right?

Miles Are we convincing?

Melanie They *are* a bit creased.

Miles Because I sometimes feel . . .

Pause.

Never mind.

Melanie Come on.

She moves him towards the door.

Miles Wait, wait.

He drags her back to the mirror.

I'll tell you something surprising . . .

That's not us . . .

Because that's not a mirror . . .

So that's not our room . . .

It's just like this one . . .

Why, what's wrong?

Lynn I just sometimes wish . . .

Pause.

I don't know . . .

Laurence I'm starving.

He moves her towards the door.

Lynn Come back.

She drags him back to the mirror.

Just suppose . . .

. . . that wasn't us.

That's a window . . .

We're looking into the next room . . .

Bed, look . . .

The irresponsibility about personal possessions . . .

And then suddenly . . .

These two.

Who are they?

Look at them . . .

Melanie We did stop the papers?

Miles No, but what do we think?

Sort of people we want to know?

Melanie You always want to

All the same things . . .

Trouser-press.

The cocktails in the Groll . . .

There in the middle of it all . . .

Two complete strangers.

Never seen them before in our lives.

Funny-looking pair.

Laurence Don't look funny to me.

Lynn Are they nice? Are they nasty?

Laurence You've got a funny way of looking at things, my pet.

see things differently from other people.

He waves at his reflection.

Miles Hello!

Melanie Come on.

Miles No, but they're waving back.

Melanie Dinner.

Miles We don't want to know you after all.

They move towards the door.

He stops.

Miles You know what's going to be going on in here while we're out?

Melanie No?

Miles No, nor do I.

She waves at her reflection.

Lynn Hello!

Laurence Come on.

Lynn Look, they want to be friends.

Laurence Eat.

Lynn Sorry, we've got to go.

They move towards the door. She stops.

Laurence Now what?

Lynn Just thinking.

Laurence Just thinking what?

Lynn What's going to be happening when we're not here?

Laurence What?

Melanie What are you talking about?

Lynn No one pressing their trousers.

Miles No one reading the notices.

She opens the door.

He opens the door.

Laurence Right, off we go.

Melanie I'm going.

Lynn No one looking at themselves in the mirror.

Miles No one looking at anything.

So what'll be happening?

Nothing will be happening.

Nothing at all.

Melanie (*to* **Laurence**) Good evening.

Laurence (*to* **Melanie**) Oh – hello.

(*To* **Miles**.) Come on. I don't want to stand there in the corridor all evening.

(*To* **Lynn**.) Buck up. There's people out here waiting to come by.

Miles Not even anything existing . . .

Lynn Nothing . . .

He shudders, switches off the lights, and goes out. The door closes. Darkness. Then it immediately re-opens, and the lights come up again as **Miles** *enters. He looks round the room. Enter* **Melanie**.

Melanie What in heaven's name is it now?

Miles Just checking.

Melanie Checking what?

Miles That it's all still here.

Melanie (*coldly*) Oh, and is it?

Miles It saw me coming.

He ushers her out, and switches off the light. Darkness. Music. Then the bedside lights come up as **Melanie** *opens the door.*

Melanie (*politely*) Good night!

Miles (*politely*) Good night!

She comes in, switching on the main lights. He follows, closing the door.

Miles Kevin and Sharon!

The original Kevin and Sharon!

He flings himself down on the bed.

She shudders, switches off the lights, and goes out. The door closes. Darkness.

Music. Then the bedside lights come up as **Laurence** *opens the door.*

Laurence (*genially*) Night night, then!

Lynn (*genially*) Sleep tight!

He comes in, switching on the main lights. She follows, closing the door.

Laurence What a Nigel!

Nigel and Nigella!

Nigel and Nigella Prat!

Why is it that one's fellow-countrymen abroad are so embarrassing?

Kind of people who make you feel ashamed to be British.

Melanie Do you want the bathroom?

Miles 'After you, Sharon.' 'Oh, ta ever so, Kevvy.'

She goes into the bathroom.

Lynn At least they were saying something to each other. At least they weren't sitting there in total silence.

She goes into the bathroom. He undresses.

Laurence No – he never stopped! Voice you can hear halfway across the restaurant. Snigger, snigger, snigger, about everything. Something funny about the music, something funny about the tablecloths. Soup doesn't come up to his high standards. They've done something comic with the fish. I thought we were never going to hear the last of the sweet trolley. And he thinks *he's* not comic? He's the comicest thing of the lot! All this sniffing the wine, all this swilling it round. You hear what he said? 'Full and fruity, with just a hint of moles' armpits.'

Lavatory flush. She comes out of the bathroom to fetch something.

Miles I think they're talking about us. Kevin and Sharon. I can hear a low indignant burbling coming through the wall.

Melanie His name's Laurence.

Miles Laurence?

Melanie She called him Laurence.

Miles Laurence . . .

Melanie Nothing funny about being called Laurence, is there?

She goes back into the bathroom.

Miles Nothing at all. Wonderful name. Saint Laurence. Laurence of Arabia . . . . What's she called?

Melanie (*off*) Lynn.

Miles Lynn? Did you say Lynn? Laurence and *Lynn*?

Lavatory flush. She comes out of the bathroom

Lynn What?

Laurence What?

Lynn I thought you said something.

Laurence I did. I said, 'Full and fruity, with just a hint of old jockstraps.'

She appears from the bathroom.

Melanie I should keep your voice down.

Miles They can't hear.

Melanie I can hear *them.*

Miles What, in the bathroom? You mean peeing?

She goes back into the bathroom.

Or worse? All right, I don't want to embarrass them. I'll call them Kevin and Sharon. I don't know how you heard they were called Laurence and Lynn. They scarcely said a word all the way through dinner. Just sat there avoiding each other's eye.

She comes out of the bathroom and undresses.

Melanie Yes, because they knew you were looking at them.

Miles I wasn't looking at them.

Melanie You obviously were.

Miles I was listening to them.

Melanie You can't have been listening to them, because you were talking all the time.

Miles *You* were listening to them.

She goes back into the bathroom.

Melanie *I* wasn't listening to them.

Miles You must have been listening to them – you heard them say something to each other. 'Oh, Laurence!' 'Oh, Lynn!' A conversation which passed me by completely, even though I was straining my ears.

Melanie She said, 'Laurence, do you want coffee?'

Miles Oh, how romantic. I'm sorry I missed that. And he replied, 'Oh, no, Lynn, no coffee for me, my precious. All I want is you.'

Melanie Aren't you going to get undressed?

Miles Ooh, Sharon, you saucy piece! I'll clean my teeth ever so quick!

He goes into the bathroom.

She comes out of the bathroom.

Laurence 'Full and fruity, with just a hint of ponces' arseholes.'

Lynn He was making a joke.

Laurence Oh, really?

Lynn It's what it said in the wine-list.

Laurence 'Just a hint of raspberries.' I know, he read it out. Twice.

Lynn Have you cleaned your teeth?

Laurence He read out most of the wine-list.

He goes into the bathroom.

Lynn I thought it was quite funny.

Laurence (*off*) I know. I saw you laugh.

Lynn I didn't laugh.

Laurence (*off*) *He* saw you laugh.

Lynn I didn't laugh!

Laurence (*off*) He was doing it for your benefit!

Lavatory flush.
She gets into bed.

Melanie I thought they were a rather sweet couple. I don't know why you have to keep putting everyone down.

Lynn I don't know why you're so cross if anything makes me laugh. I thought they seemed a nice couple.

At least he didn't keep talking all the time, he didn't keep making jokes. They could just sit there in peace.

At least he was saying something. At least he was making a few jokes. They could sit there and have a good time together.

I don't know why you can't just quietly enjoy things for a moment.

She gets into bed.

I wish *you'd* got a bit more sense of humour.

Laurence *comes out of the bathroom, cleaning his teeth.*

Laurence You telling me I haven't got a sense of humour?

Lynn Well, you're not a *great* one for jokes, are you?

Laurence Jokes? You want jokes? There's this feller goes into a bar . . .

Lynn Stop cleaning your teeth for a moment, then.

Laurence There's this feller goes into a bar. Right?

Lynn Right.

Laurence No, there's this feller sitting in a bar, and this feller comes in, this other feller.

Lynn Why don't you have a little practice on your own first?

Laurence Feller walks up the wall, right? Feller who's come in. Feller watches him. Feller in the bar. Feller walks across the ceiling. OK? Walks down the other wall and out of the bar. Feller in the bar says: 'That's

Miles *comes out of the bathroom.*

Miles The imagination boggles at what old Kevin's up in that bathroom.

Melanie What are you talking about?

Miles Cleans his teeth, then flushes the loo. I know people get a little confused about the functions of the *bidet*, but cleaning your teeth in the lavatory . . . .

He undresses.

Melanie Will you do something?

Miles What do you want?

Melanie We're on holiday.

Miles Yes?

Melanie Special treat. For me.

Miles OK.

Melanie Say something serious.

funny, he didn't say Good evening.'

Lynn You've got toothpaste on your chin.

Laurence The *barman* says: 'That's funny, he didn't say Good evening.'

Lynn Have you flushed?

He goes back into the bathroom. Lavatory flush.

Miles All right.

Melanie Just one thing.

Miles One thing . . . Anything?

Melanie Anything.

Miles Bright's Disease.

Melanie Thank you.

He gets into bed.

Miles I expect old Kevin's being serious.

Laurence *comes out of the bathroom.*

Laurence *Dog* walks into a bar . . .

Lynn Light.

Laurence Says to the barman . . .

Lynn Light. In the bathroom. It's on.

He turns out the bathroom light.

Laurence You'd better move in with Nigel, then. I expect *he's* telling jokes.

He puts his ear to the wall.

Miles Gone very quiet in there.

He puts his ear to the wall.

Melanie What are you doing?

Lynn What are you doing?

Laurence (*voice down*) No one

Miles (*voice down*) Bit of serious whispering going on.

Melanie That's a horrible thing to do.

Miles Sh!

He's saying something . . .

'Oh, Sharon, I love you!'

He takes his head away from the wall and gazes at it in mock surprise.

He reapplies his ear to the wall.

'Oh, Kevin, I love you, too!'

He starts away from the wall again in mock surprise.

He puts his ear back to the wall, and starts away again in genuine surprise.

Miles Good God.

saying anything at all in there, I'll tell you that.

Bit of whispering, that's all.

Lynn I don't think that's very nice.

Laurence Sh!

What's he saying?

He takes his head away from the wall and gazes at it in surprise.

Lynn What?

He reapplies his ear to the wall.

He starts away from the wall again. He laughs.

Lynn What? What's going on?

Laurence No sense of humour? What about this, then? Old Nigel and Nigella in there . . .

He laughs.

Melanie Why? What's happening?

Miles (*disconcerted*) Laughing his head off.

He turns out the light. Darkness. Pause. Lights on again. He is sitting up in bed, looking round the room.

Melanie Now what?

Miles Just checking.

He turns the lights out again. Darkness.

Miles You know I love you?

Lynn What? What?

Laurence Know what they're called? Kevin and Sharon!

He turns out the light. Darkness.

Laurence Kevin and Sharon!

Lynn Very funny.

Laurence All right – tell you something else, then.

Lynn No more jokes tonight.

Laurence No, something serious.

Lynn Bit of sleep first.

Pause.

Laurence I love you.

Pause.

I said I love you.

Lynn Um.

Pause.

Melanie (*coolly*) Do you?

Miles You know I do. It's the Kevin and Sharon story all over again.

Melanie Oh.

Miles No, I'm saying something serious. I'm trying to say something serious. I *am* saying something serious.

Melanie Oh, good.

Miles So how about you?

Melanie What?

Miles Do you love me?

Melanie Yes.

Miles Yes?

Melanie I've said – yes!

Lights on.

Melanie Now what?

Miles Just checking.

Melanie Do stop this!

Miles No, the expression on your face when you say that.

She turns out the light.

Lynn Laurence? You're not asleep, are you?

Laurence Um?

Lynn Laurence . . .

Laurence What's the matter?

Lynn I love you, too.

Lights on. He is sitting up in bed looking at her.

Miles 'Yes?' Just – 'yes'?

Melanie What are you talking about?

Miles I say, 'Do you love me?' And you just say 'yes', and turn out the lights?

Pause. Then she turns over and embraces him.

Pause. Lights on. She is sitting up in bed.

Laurence What? I said! I said before!

Lynn Mosquito.

Laurence Mosquito?

Lynn I heard it.

Laurence I can't hear anything.

Lynn I heard it!

Laurence Gone.

Lynn It'll be back.

Laurence Get some sleep.

Lynn Soon as we put the lights out.

She puts the lights out.

Laurence Not a sound.

Lynn I'm listening.

Laurence Go to sleep.

Lynn I'm waiting.

Melanie Come on, then.

Miles I didn't mean that.

Melanie Yes, you did. Come on. Quietly, though.

Miles Quietly, right.

Melanie Don't wake the whole hotel.

Miles Don't want to make Kevin and Sharon jealous.

Lights on. She is sitting up in bed, slapping at herself.

Lynn Get off! Get off!

Laurence What, back?

Lynn I felt it go in! Look, blood! There's blood on the sheet!

Oh dear. Bit of competition.

Melanie Never mind them. Go on if you're going to.

There! There!

She jumps up on the bed, pointing at the ceiling, and pulls the duvet round her. He gets to his feet.

Laurence Where?

Lynn There!

He fetches a towel, and attempts to track the mosquito as it moves about the room.

Up here . . . ! Down there . . . ! No . . . Yes!

Laurence Oh, right . . . You little devil!

He enters into the spirit of the chase.

Lynn Give me another one . . .

He hands her another towel.

Laurence Here!

Slaps the towel at it.

Lynn There!

Slaps.

Laurence Where?

They rain a fusillade of slaps.

Miles What – flagellation?

Melanie Don't listen.

Miles Don't listen?

Lynn Nearly!

Laurence Wor!

Lynn Careful!

Laurence Wallop! Wallop!

Lynn Wait, wait . . . Now!

Laurence Ah!

Lynn Yes! No . . .

They pause, panting, searching.

Miles We should have guessed. They look so abnormally normal . . .

Melanie They've finished.

Miles Have they?

Melanie Go on.

Miles I'm listening.

Melanie Silence.

Miles Right . . .

Miles *reaches for the light switch.*

Melanie No?

Miles No.

He turns out the light.
Music, as before. The crash of a tablelamp falling over.

Melanie (*sleepily*) What's happening?

Miles Nothing. Go back to sleep.

Melanie Turn on the light.

They both cry out, pointing at the ceiling over the bed. They jump wildly about all over the bed, grunting and shouting, trying to reach the mosquito as it moves around the ceiling.

Laurence Gotcher!

Lynn Gotcher!

Laurence Very satisfactory.

Lynn That's my blood on the ceiling.

They settle down in bed.

Laurence Know what?

Lynn What?

Laurence I enjoyed that.

He turns out the light.
Music, as before.

Miles That *was* the light.

More noises in the darkness.

Melanie What time is it?

Miles Quarter past three.

Melanie What are you doing?

Miles Trying not to disturb you.

Pause. Then a crash, a cry of pain, and the noise of a gunfight, very loud. Dramatic music. Shouts in Rewindese.

Melanie Oh, my God!

He turns out the light.

He is on his hands and knees in his suitcase.

Melanie What in the name of heaven . . . ?

Miles Suitcase!

Melanie You've turned the TV on!

Miles I fell on the remote!

Melanie Turn it off!

Miles I'm trying to! I can't find it!

He turns on the light.

Laurence There's a riot going on!

Not the car? They're not attacking the car?

He jumps out of bed and hurries to the window to look.

Melanie You'll wake the whole hotel!

Lynn It's next door! They've gone mad!

She hammers on the wall.

It's next door! You've woken them up!

He hunts through spilled clothes.

Miles I can't find the remote!

You'll have to go and talk to them!

He storms out of the door, followed by her.

Melanie What's this?

She retrieves the remote.

Miles That's it!

Thundering on the door. He goes to open it.

Melanie Which button?

Miles The top one!

The sound redoubles in intensity, as **Miles** *opens the door.* **Laurence** *stands on the threshold, with* **Lynn** *behind him.*

Laurence Look, I'm sorry, but it's three o'clock in the morning . . . !

Miles I know, I know! (*To* **Melanie**.) The top one, the top one!

The sound redoubles in intensity again. **Miles** *comes hurrying back to help, followed by* **Laurence** *and* **Lynn**.

The bottom one!

The sound switches to low-grade Rewindese porn, hugely loud.

Oh my God . . . ! The blue one! The red one!

Lynn (*screams*) The one that says 'off'!

Silence. Pause.

Miles I'm so sorry.

Laurence I thought we'd got a riot going on!

Miles I am most abjectly apologetic.

Lynn He thought it was the car! He thought they'd got the cars!

Miles I fell on the remote. I do most humbly and contritely apologise.

Melanie But . . . what were you *doing*?

Miles I was trying not to disturb you.

Melanie I know. But . . .

Miles Looking for the bathroom.

He feels along the downstage left wall to demonstrate.

Couldn't find the door.

Melanie The bathroom's over here!

She points to it, upstage. **Miles** *looks at it, then back at the downstage left wall.*

Miles It was here last night.

Laurence Well, if you're OK . . .

Laurence *and* **Lynn** *execute a withdrawal.*

Melanie I'm terribly sorry.

Miles Extremely sorry.

Lynn No, sorry to come bursting in.

Melanie Very sorry.

Laurence No, only it's three o'clock in the morning . . .

Miles Dreadfully sorry.

He closes the door. Pause.

Melanie I'll put it up here. The remote. You won't fall on it up here?

She gets back into bed.

Laurence *and* **Lynn** *enter.*

Lynn Moved the bathroom? And then he turns the telly on? At three o'clock in the morning? *What* are they called?

Laurence (*shortly*) Kevin and Sharon.

Lynn Very funny pair. You're right.

I *told* you not to leave the suitcase there.

Miles Last night the suitcase was *here*. The bathroom was *there* . . .

Melanie Aren't you going, then? After all that?

Miles *This* was the suitcase – *that* was the bathroom.

She lies down and turns away from him.

Miles Turn the light out, then.

He goes into the bathroom.

Melanie What, and start all over again?

Miles (*off*) I'm there now. Go back to sleep!

Melanie It's not anything to laugh about, you know. Waking everyone up. Spoiling their holiday. Making a complete fool of yourself.

They get back into bed.

I said you're right.

Laurence I heard you.

Lynn I thought you'd be laughing.

Laurence Did you?

He turns off the light.

She turns on the light.

Lynn Go on, then.

Laurence What?

Lynn What have I done wrong?

Laurence What do you mean?

Lynn I've done something wrong. I've said the wrong thing.

Laurence Let's get some sleep.

He turns the light out. She turns the light on.

Lynn What was it?

Laurence Forget it.

He turns the light out. She turns the light on.

Lynn What, the car? Because I said about the car?

Laurence *Someone's* got to think about the car!

Lynn Fine, good, think about the car, nobody's stopping you!

Laurence You don't have to go shouting it out to everyone in the world!

He comes out of the bathroom.

Miles I said turn out the light. If you want to go to sleep.

He turns the light out.

She sits up in bed.

Melanie I feel very embarrassed.

Miles *You* feel embarrassed?

Melanie You're always doing this kind of thing.

Miles I have never before mistaken the position of a hotel bathroom.

Melanie You've fallen over your suitcase.

Miles But never on to the remote control of a television set.

Melanie You're always . . . shouting . . . and making jokes . . . and crashing about . . . !

Miles Sh!

Melanie Are *you* shushing *me*?

He gestures at her to keep her voice down.

You think they've got back to sleep after all that? I'll tell you what they're doing. They're talking about us.

She turns the light on.

Lynn What, you think they're lying there talking about you?

Laurence I don't care what they're doing.

Miles I might have expected a bit of sympathy, a bit of

loyalty. I could have broken my leg.

I do in fact have a rather painful bruise on my elbow. Never mind, though. Sleep well.

He lies down and turns his back.

Melanie I wonder if *he* treats *her* like this?

She turns out the light. Darkness. A phrase of music. Then grey light – pink light – dawn.

Miles *sits up.*

Miles (*alarmed*) Where are we?

Melanie (*wakes*) What? What is it?

Miles I can't remember which country we're in!

Melanie Don't start.

Miles Oh yes. It's the Place with the Trouser-press.

He gets up, and orients himself.

I just don't like you shooting your mouth off about me to all and sundry.

He lies down and turns his back.

Lynn I wonder if *he* treats *her* like this?

She turns out the light. Darkness. A phrase of music. Then grey light – pink light – dawn.

She sits up.

Lynn (*alarmed*) What time is it?

She finds her watch.

Lynn (*looking at her watch*) Are we ahead or are we behind?

Trouser-press . . . suitcase . . . car-park . . .

He looks round carefully.

Miles Bathroom! All right?

Melanie I said, Don't start.

He goes into the bathroom. She gets up.

What sort of day is it?

She goes out on to the balcony.

He gets up and heads straight for the window.

Lynn What, the car?

Laurence What?

Lynn You're going to look at the car?

Laurence I'm on my way to the bathroom.

He diverts sharply to the bathroom.

All right?

She gets up.

Lynn (*concessive*) Don't worry. *I'll* have a look.

She goes out on to the balcony.

Melanie Oh. Sorry!

Lynn Sorry!

Melanie *goes back inside again.* **Lynn** *gazes down at the car-park.* **Melanie** *goes out on to the balcony again.*

Melanie Sorry about all the performance in the night.

Lynn Oh, no. We just didn't know what was happening. He thought it was the revolution breaking out.

Melanie I was so embarrassed.

Lynn No, mine's just as bad. Night before last, middle of the night, he gets up, and yes, he finds the bathroom, no problem, but then what happens? – I don't know – he won't turn the light on – he starts crashing about – I say 'For heaven's sake turn the light on!' – he *won't* turn the light on – next thing I know everything's going smash, crash . . . I go running in – the floor's covered in broken glass – and he starts shouting at *me* – somehow it's all *my* fault!

She peers.

Melanie What – your car?

Lynn See if it's all right. I got into hot water over that, too. Shouldn't have said he was worried about it. He was *furious*!

Melanie *He* was furious! I don't know what *he'd* got to be furious about. I *told* him not to leave his suitcase there!

Lynn Wouldn't speak, mine!

Melanie I quite like it when they won't speak.

Lynn *peers.* **Melanie** *looks as well.*

Melanie Which one is it?

Lynn I can't remember.

Melanie What colour is it?

Lynn I've forgotten. What colour's yours?

Melanie Search me.

Lynn I don't know what we're doing here, tell you the truth.

Melanie *I* don't know what we're doing here!

Lynn I don't know where we're going!

Melanie *I* don't know where we're going!

Lynn *He* dreamed all this up!

Melanie Supposed to be a break for me.

Lynn I'd rather put my feet up with a good book.

Melanie I just want to get on with my work.

Lynn I suppose *they* like it.

Melanie Do they?

Lynn Don't they?

Melanie Not much evidence of it.

Lynn He gets in such a state about it.

Melanie He never wants to *meet* anyone.

Lynn Never wants to *meet* anyone!

They realise that **Laurence** *and* **Miles** *have come out of the bathroom, and are watching them.*

Melanie Oh, here he is.

Lynn He's giving me a very funny look.

Melanie He'll think we're talking about him.

Lynn They always think you're talking about them!

Melanie See you in breakfast, perhaps.

Lynn *and* **Melanie** *go back inside.*

Miles So how's Sharon this morning?

Melanie Fine.

Miles Telling you all about Kevin?

Melanie Have you finished in the bathroom?

Miles Or were you telling her all about me?

Melanie What colour's our car?

Miles They haven't broken into it?

Melanie I said what colour is it?

Miles They haven't *taken* it?

He goes out on to the balcony.

Laurence So how's the car?

Lynn The car?

Laurence I thought you were looking at the car?

Lynn The car's fine.

He goes out on to the balcony.

Lynn Don't you believe me?

Laurence See what sort of day it is . . .

Laurence Oh – hello!

Miles Sorry – just checking the car's still there.

Laurence OK?

Miles Seems to be. Yours all right?

Laurence Hadn't thought. Let's have a look. Yes, still there. Still got four wheels.

Miles Sorry about . . . you know . . . in the night.

Laurence No, I sympathise. Diabolical, the way they move the bathrooms around in these places. You'd think they'd standardise. You'd think

Brussels would do something.

Miles Have the same layout everywhere.

Laurence By law.

Miles TV here, bathroom there.

Laurence You find the bathroom – you *still* don't know where you are. One night you've got the basin here, you've got the loo there. Next night – the basin's here, the loo's there.

Miles You get up in the middle of the night . . .

Laurence Night before last. Don't want to disturb *her* . . .

Miles So you don't turn the light on . . .

Laurence Don't turn the light on. And there I am in the bathroom, bending down . . .

Miles Feeling for the loo . . .

Laurence Feeling for the loo . . .

Miles Which in fact is behind you . . .

Laurence Which in fact is behind me . . .

Miles So your head . . .

Laurence Unknown to me . . .

Miles Is in the basin.

Laurence Suddenly . . .

Miles Thump!

Laurence Hot tap – *here*, over my right eye.

Miles Right eye?

Laurence Right eye. Jump up . . .

Miles Don't tread on the remote . . .

Laurence Don't tread on the remote, no,

because the remote's not in the bathroom. Worse. Hit the back of my head against the shelf over the basin.

Miles Crack!

Laurence Glass shelf.

Miles Of course.

Laurence Not fixed.

Miles Certainly not.

Laurence Loose on its brackets.

Miles Naturally.

Laurence Plus various glass tumblers, pots of face cream et cetera, make-up mirror et cetera et cetera.

Miles Glass everywhere.

Laurence All over the floor.

Miles Bare feet.

Laurence In the dark.

Miles Your wife comes running.

Laurence 'What are you playing at?'

Miles 'You'll wake the whole hotel!'

Laurence 'Don't come in! Don't move! Just turn the light on!'

Miles 'Where's the light?'

Laurence 'Can't find the light!'

Miles Total panic.

Laurence They should standardise the light switches.

Miles Put your hand out, no matter where you are.

Laurence Spain, France, Luxembourg.

Miles On comes the light.

Laurence I mean, it wasn't my idea in the first place.

Miles Going on holiday?

Laurence I'd just as soon do the garden, quite frankly.

Miles I shouldn't mind working, to tell you the truth. I quite like working.

Laurence But you put yourself out.

Miles Whatever you do you know it's not going to be right.

Laurence Ah well.

Miles There you go.

Laurence What would we do without them?

Miles Holidays?

Laurence No . . .

He nods in the direction of the room. **Lynn** *and* **Melanie** *are packing, and watching* **Laurence** *and* **Miles** *curiously.*

Miles Oh. Yes. Right. What indeed?

Laurence Bless their hearts.

Miles Anyway, you got back to sleep in the end?

Laurence Out like a light. You and Sharon?

Miles Me and . . . ?

Laurence Sharon? Got a bit of sleep?

Miles Oh – us – yes. Fine, fine.

Laurence Well, better go and shave.

Miles On into the great unknown.

Laurence Wonder where the bathroom'll be tonight?

Miles Touch of mystery to our lives.

Laurence See you in breakfast?

Miles Yes, you must meet Sharon.

Laurence Been nice talking to you, Kevin.

Miles *and* **Laurence** *go back into their rooms.*

Melanie (*coolly*) I'm glad you've found someone to talk to at last.

Miles Me and Kevin? We're like that together.

Lynn (*coolly*) Well, you seem to have found a soul-mate.

Laurence What, old Kevin? He's all right.

We're having breakfast with them.

Thought we might all meet up over breakfast.

Lynn Oh, well, this is a change.

She goes into the bathroom.

'We've all done it, Kevin. We've all been there. We've all had troubles with the bathroom. Women, Kevin? They're all alike.'

Melanie (*shocked*) You didn't call him Kevin?

Miles I didn't call him Kevin. *He* called *me* Kevin.

Melanie *He* called *you* Kevin?

Miles 'You and Sharon get back to sleep all right, Kevin?' You're Sharon.

Melanie He called me Sharon?

Miles He wants to meet you properly over breakfast. Two Kevins – two Sharons – we're going to get on like a house on fire.

She gazes at him in horror.

Melanie He heard you! Everything you said about them! He heard you!

She comes out of the bathroom, holding toilet stuff to pack.

Lynn Well, just as long as you don't go calling him Kevin.

Laurence What do you want me to call him? Nigel?

Lynn You didn't . . . ?

Laurence Didn't what?

Lynn Call him Kevin just now? You didn't call him Kevin out there?

Laurence Kevin, yes. Why not? Kevin. What's wrong?

She gazes at him in horror.

Lynn He *told* you he's called Kevin?

Laurence I *know* he's called Kevin!

Come on – finish packing! Let's get out of here!

Miles Breakfast . . .

Melanie I couldn't look them in the eye!

Miles Come on – be reasonable.

Melanie I *am* being reasonable!

Miles We'll make a joke of it.

Melanie *They've* made the joke of it already. Somebody else making the jokes for once. Close your case up.

She hurls together the last of the packing.

Quick, before we meet them in the corridor!

Lynn Because you were listening through the wall, you turnip!

She hurls together the last of the packing.

We'll get breakfast on the road somewhere.

Laurence We've paid for breakfast here.

Lynn What, and sit there with Kevin and Sharon, and them knowing we've had our ear to the wall?

Come on, or we'll be meeting them in the corridor!

That the lot?	
	Have we got everything?
Come on.	
They open the door, and struggle out with their luggage.	*They open the door, and struggle out with their luggage.*
	Buck up, buck up!
Oh, hello!	
	Hello!
Miles Thought we'd give breakfast a miss, after all.	
	Laurence Us, too.
Hit the road.	
	Beat the traffic.
Melanie Hold on. Just check we've got everything . . .	
	Lynn See if we've left anything behind . . .
She pushes him back into the room, and closes the door.	*She pushes him back into the room, and closes the door.*
Miles What?	**Laurence** What?
	Lynn Let them get out of the way first.
Melanie Give them a head start.	
Miles I don't know why *they're* going.	**Laurence** I don't know why *they're* going.
Melanie (*grimly*) Don't you?	**Lynn** (*grimly*) Don't you?
They wait.	*They wait. She listens at the door.*
	Laurence (*looks round the room*) Bit of our life.

Miles (*looks round the room*) And so another chapter in the story closes behind us.

No sign we were ever here.

Melanie The lampshade wasn't that shape when we arrived . . .

They wait.

Miles They must have gone by now.

Actually, if they've gone . . .

We could have breakfast.

Melanie Don't be silly.

Miles Leave now, we'll bump into them in the car-park.

Pause. She puts her case down.

Lynn What?

Laurence I said it's a bit of our life. This room.

Lynn I know.

Laurence Haven't left anything?

Lynn Bit of my lifeblood up there on the ceiling . . .

They wait.

Laurence Listen . . . Silence.

If they've gone . . .

We could have breakfast.

Lynn I just want to get out of here.

Laurence They'll still be paying their bill.

Pause. She puts her case down.

Melanie Quickly, then . . .

Miles Breakfast?

She flings the door open and goes out, then bundles him back inside again.

Melanie Why do I ever listen to anything you say?

She picks up the bags.

Miles If they're still . . .

Melanie Out, out, out, out!

They go straight out with all the luggage.

Melanie (*merrily*) Change of plan!

Miles You too?

Melanie Never get away from each other again!

Miles *and* **Melanie** (*together*) Doomed to be doubles!

They cast one last haggard look back into the room, then go out, laughing, and close the door. Darkness.

Lynn Breakfast.

She flings the door open and goes out, then bundles him back inside again.

I knew it, I knew it!

She picks up the bags.

Come on!

Laurence But . . .

Lynn I don't care! Just get out of here!

They go straight out with all the luggage.

Lynn (*merrily*) Change of plan!

Laurence You too?

Lynn Never get away from each other again!

Laurence *and* **Lynn** (*together*) Doomed to be doubles!

They cast one last haggard look back into the room, then go out, laughing, and close the door. Darkness.

Act Two

Leavings

Table and chairs. **John, Jocasta, Nicholas** *and* **Nancy**.

Nancy*'s arm is in a sling.* **John** *is asleep.*

Pause.

Nicholas Well . . .

Nancy Well . . .

Pause.

Jocasta Shall I make some more coffee?

Nicholas No, we really ought to be . . .

Nancy (*looks at her watch*) Oh, my God, yes – look at the time!

Nicholas (*looks at his watch*) How did it get to be so late?

Pause.

Nancy We were going to be going half an hour ago.

Nicholas Yes – how come we're still sitting here?

Pause.

Nancy Well, then . . .

Nicholas (*looks at* **John**) We must let these good people get some sleep.

Jocasta (*to* **John**) Darling . . .

Nicholas Don't wake him.

Nancy Busy day.

Nicholas Privilege of the host.

Nancy We'll just quietly slip away.

Pause.

Jocasta You don't have to go dashing off.

Nicholas Some of us have got to get up in the morning.

Pause.

Jocasta Well, if you've really got to . . .

Nicholas Come on, then.

Nancy Lovely evening.

Nicholas *and* **Nancy** *push their chairs back.*

Jocasta (*nudges* **John**; *firmly*) Darling . . . They're leaving . . .

John (*wakes up*) Yes, we've got to be going. (*Looks at his watch.*) Oh my God, look at the time!

Jocasta Darling!

John How did it get to be so late? Some of us have got to get up in the morning! Come on, then.

He gets to his feet.

Lovely evening. We must let these good people get some sleep . . .

He stops, confused.

Jocasta Honestly!

Nicholas Well, if you've really got to . . .

John No, no . . .

Nicholas We mustn't stop you.

Jocasta You live here. Remember?

John No, no, no, no . . .

Jocasta What do mean, no, no, no, no?

Nancy Don't worry! We can take a hint!

Nicholas *and* **Nancy** *get to their feet.*

John I mean, *you* sit down! Go on – sit down, sit down, sit down, sit down! Have another glass of wine!

He refills their glasses.

Jocasta They were just going!

John Nonsense! Sit down!

Nicholas It's taken us an hour to get on our feet.

John Sit down!

Nicholas You slept through the entire negotiations!

John I wasn't asleep!

Nicholas He wasn't asleep.

John I was thinking.

Nicholas Deep in thought.

John About what you were saying. Sit down!

Nicholas What *were* we saying?

Nancy We weren't saying anything.

Nicholas Long silences.

Nancy While we were waiting for *you* to speak.

Nicholas That's how we knew it was time to go.

John About machines.

Nicholas About machines?

John About burglar alarms and answering machines.

Nicholas Oh, that!

Nancy Then!

Jocasta That was when we got back from casualty!

Nancy Was that this evening?

Nicholas Good God, have you been asleep since then?

John What you were saying . . .

Nancy Bye bye.

Kisses him.

Thank you so much. I'm sorry about the . . . (*Indicates her arm.*)

Jocasta No – all our fault.

Nancy Don't come out.

Exit **Nancy** *left, followed by* **Jocasta**.

John What you were saying . . .

Nicholas Listen, we'll continue this another time.

John . . . was that there was something unnatural about our dependence on all these machines.

Nicholas Very enjoyable evening. Though actually that isn't what I was saying.

John Oh, I thought it was.

Nicholas We can't start all this again now, but as a matter of fact *you* were saying it was unnatural.

John *You* were saying it was unnatural, and I was saying, no, what would be unnatural, now that these machines have been invented, now that they're actually in existence, would be *not* to use them.

Nicholas No, what I was saying, what I was trying to say, was that it was very *natural* to use them . . .

John 'Unnatural' was the word you actually employed.

Nicholas No, what I actually said was that it was only *too* natural . . .

John Only too natural – exactly.

Nicholas Only too natural doesn't mean unnatural.

John Of course it does. Only too natural means *unnaturally* natural.

Nicholas Unnaturally natural? This is an interesting concept . . .

He sits down.

John What's odd about something being unnaturally natural?

Nicholas What's odd about something being unnaturally natural? Look . . . Sit down, sit down.

John *sits.*

Nicholas Supposing I said something was naturally unnatural.

Enter **Nancy** *left.*

John You might well say that.

Nancy Oh no!

John Something might well be naturally unnatural.

Nancy You haven't sat down again?

Nicholas Give me an example of something naturally unnatural.

Enter **Jocasta** *left.*

John This table is naturally unnatural.

Jocasta They've sat down again!

John This glass is naturally unnatural.

Nancy I thought we were going?

John This chair is naturally unnatural.

Nancy Come on!

Nicholas You mean it's unnatural by nature?

John I mean it's unnatural by nature.

Nicholas Like an answering machine or a burglar alarm?

Nancy *sits down in exasperation.*

Nicholas Don't start sitting down again! (*To* **John**.) Like an answering machine or a burglar alarm? (*To* **Nancy**.) I thought we were going?

Nancy *gets up.*

Nicholas (*to* **John**) I thought you were arguing that they were natural?

Nancy *forces Nicholas up and propels him towards the door.* **John** *follows.*

John Yes! Naturally natural!

Nicholas But now you're saying they're naturally unnatural!

John No, I'm not – I'm saying they're not unnaturally natural! No – not unnaturally unnatural . . . No, hold on . . .

Nicholas I don't know what we're talking about.

John *I* don't know what we're talking about.

Exit **Nicholas** *and* **John** *left.* **Nancy** *turns back to* **Jocasta.**

Nancy Sorry. First they won't say anything . . .

Jocasta Then they won't stop.

Nancy I know – I meant to ask you about Ariadne . . .

Exit **Nancy** *left.* **Jocasta** *stops.*

Jocasta You haven't heard?

Enter **Nancy** *left.*

Nancy Heard what?

Jocasta About Ariadne!

Nancy No?

Jocasta She's left Reggie.

Nancy Left Reggie? Ariadne has left Reggie?

Jocasta According to Joanna.

Nancy What – somebody else?

Jocasta You'll never guess! Grantley Forward!

Nancy Grantley Forward? Reggie . . . and Grantley Forward?

Jocasta Ariadne and Grantley Forward!

Nancy No!

Jocasta Yes!

Nancy But I thought Grantley . . .

Jocasta With Georgina, yes. But you know that Georgina . . .

Nancy And Luciano . . .

Jocasta For years!

Nancy For years!

Jocasta Well, apparently he came back unexpectedly one day . . .

Enter **Nicholas** *left, and waits with ostentatious patience.*

Nancy Luciano?

Jocasta Grantley! And found the two of them manacled to the bed together!

Nancy Luciano and Georgina?

Jocasta No!

Nicholas John's standing on the pavement out there. They'll arrest him for loitering.

Nancy Georgina and *Reggie*?

Jocasta Amanda and Laurence!

Nancy Amanda and Laurence? Who are they?

Jocasta No one knows!

Nicholas *takes* **Nancy** *by the arm.*

Nicholas It's like getting the couple in the weather house outdoors at the same time.

He kisses **Jocasta**.

Nancy Amanda and Laurence?

Nicholas No, no! Good night. Thank you so much. Loved the bit in casualty.

Exit **Nicholas** *and* **Nancy** *left.*

Nancy (*off*) But I don't understand . . .

Jocasta (*calls*) I'll give you a ring in the morning. Night night! Love to Charlie and Georgie!

Jocasta *yawns. Enter* **Nicholas** *left. She stops yawning.*

Nicholas You know Charlie got ninety-eight per cent in maths?

Jocasta Yes, Nancy said!

Nicholas He was so cross about it, though! He said, 'Dad, I got one wrong.' And when he showed me the paper . . .

Jocasta It was the the teacher who'd got it wrong!

Nicholas Sorry, sorry.

Jocasta No, no – nice to hear it confirmed. Night night.

Exit **Nicholas** *left. Enter* **Nicholas** *left, guiltily.*

Nicholas And Theodora? I meant to ask earlier.

Jocasta She's doing very well.

Nicholas The remedial reading . . . ?

Jocasta Is really helping. We're terribly pleased.

Enter **John** *left.*

John Have you two separated?

Nicholas Sorry. I was just asking about Theodora.

John What, this remedial caper?

Nicholas I gather it's really doing the trick.

John Yes – she can read quite long words now.

Nicholas Marvellous!

John Like the 'Play' on the video.

Jocasta She can read *all* the video controls.

John Except 'Stop'. She can't read 'Stop'.

Nicholas Anyway . . .

Jocasta What she needs is you to believe in what she's doing.

John What she needs is everyone to stop fussing.

Enter **Nancy** *left.*

Nancy You can see the stars moving out there if you watch for long enough.

Jocasta Sorry. We're talking about Theodora.

Nancy Oh, right.

John I mean, it's ridiculous. Some people are *natural* slow readers.

Nicholas *Naturally* natural slow readers?

John *Naturally* natural slow readers – yes.

Nancy I'll sit down.

She sits.

Nicholas Don't sit down! We're going, we're going!

Jocasta (*to* **Nicholas**) No, but bear me out! It's *not* natural not to be reading at her age! It's highly unnatural!

John It's not natural to read at any age!

Jocasta Oh, for heaven's sake!

John Reading is a highly unnatural activity.

Nicholas A *naturally* unnatural activity?

John A *naturally* unnatural activity.

Jocasta Oh, don't start all that again!

John But it is!

Jocasta Come on!

Exit **Jocasta** *left.*

John In fact it's an *unnaturally* unnatural activity . . .

Exit **John** *left.*

Nicholas You're still sitting there!

Nancy I want to be absolutely certain you're outside that door before I get to my feet.

Nicholas You're the one who keeps coming back!

Nancy Come on.

Nicholas It would make more sense . . .

He sits.

. . . if I stayed sitting down until *you* were outside that door.

Enter **Jocasta** *left. She gazes at* **Nicholas** *and* **Nancy** *in astonishment.*

Jocasta What?

Nicholas We're waiting.

Jocasta Waiting? What for?

Nancy Each other.

Nicholas Together. All right?

Nancy All right – together.

They get to their feet, watching each other. **Jocasta** *watches them.*

Nicholas Go on.

Nancy Together, yes?

Nicholas We can't get through the door together.

Nancy After you, then.

Nicholas After you.

Nancy Go on.

Nicholas No, no.

Jocasta *I'll* go.

Exit **Jocasta** *left.*

Nancy (*to* **Jocasta**) We're going to end up like those two manacled to the bed.

Exit **Nancy**.

Nicholas What, Laurence Troon and Amanda Wivenhoe?

Enter **Nancy** *left.*

Nancy It was Laurence *Troon?* And Amanda *Wivenhoe?*

Nicholas According to George Worrall.

Nancy You said you didn't know!

Nicholas I didn't say anything.

Nancy But this is terrible!

She pushes the door to.

Nicholas What? What's happening?

Nancy Amanda Wivenhoe lives with Charlie's maths tutor!

Nicholas Yes, but he can't really complain. He's also involved with that Kung Fu woman in Huddersfield . . .

Nancy But if Charlie's maths tutor finds out about Amanda and Laurence Troon . . .

She sits down.

. . . and moves in with the Kung Fu woman . . .

Nicholas In Huddersfield . . . ?

Nancy Then who do we get to tutor Charlie?

Nicholas Oh my God!

He sits down.

Nancy He doesn't know about Laurence Troon so far?

Nicholas I've no idea.

Nancy Who told you?

Nicholas George Worrall.

Enter **Jocasta** *and* **John** *left.*

Nancy Who presumably got it from Patsy.

Nicholas Who will have told Clarissa.

Nancy Who knows the Pillingtons.

Nicholas Who may meet Charlie's maths tutor at the Muldews . . .

Nancy We must make absolutely sure it doesn't go any further.

Nicholas I won't tell a soul.

Nancy Not a soul!

Nicholas Not a soul!

John Sorry. We just happened to be outside. Saw the front door was open – thought we'd drop in . . .

Nancy Yes, sit down, sit down!

Nicholas You're not going to believe this . . .

Nancy (*to* **Nicholas**) Not a *soul*!

Nicholas Not a *soul*!

Nancy It was Laurence Troon and Amanda Wivenhoe!

Jocasta You mean . . . ?

Nancy Yes!

Jocasta No!

She sits. **John** *watches them.*

Nicholas And Amanda Wivenhoe lives with Charlie's maths tutor!

Nancy Who's also involved with this woman in Huddersfield . . .

Nicholas Who teaches Kung Fu!

Nancy Who teaches Kung Fu!

Nicholas So what's going to happen?

Nancy He's going to leave Amanda . . .

Nicholas And go zooming up to Huddersfield!

John Laurence Troon?

Nancy
Nicholas
Jocasta } Charlie's maths tutor!

John (*resignedly*) Oh, Charlie's maths tutor.

He sits.

Nancy Another glass of wine?

Nicholas Or something to eat?

Nancy I feel suddenly kind of hollow inside.

John How about breakfast?

Nicholas I'll do it!

Nancy I'll do it!

Nicholas Scrambled eggs?

Nancy A bit of bacon?

Jocasta Well . . .

John Actually . . .

Nicholas No, no!

Nancy You sit there . . .

Nicholas . . . and make yourselves at home . . . !

Curtain.

Look Away Now

Three aircraft seats.

Three passengers sitting in them: **Aptly, Bloss** *and* **Charr**.

Reassuring music. It suddenly stops.

Stewardess (*off, over PA*) Now will you please ensure that your seat belt is securely fastened, ready for take-off.

Passengers **Aptly** *and* **Charr** *gaze absently and expressionlessly into space.* **Charr** *yawns. Passenger* **Bloss,** *between them, automatically checks the items mentioned.*

Stewardess Your table should be folded away, with the seat-back upright and the arm-rest down. Your mind should be in the closed position to be adopted when routine safety announcements of this sort are made.

Aptly *glances at him, and he stops.*

Stewardess If you are still conscious at this time, you may find the level tone of voice in which this announcement is being made helpful in securing complete inattention. In the pocket in front of you you will find a card showing aircraft safety procedures.

Bloss *automatically moves to look for the card.* **Aptly** *glances at him again, and he sits back and gazes into space.*

Stewardess In the interest of your own peace of mind, please studiously ignore this. Any attempt to look at it may result in your appearing nervous or inexperienced to your fellow-passengers. We are mentioning it purely as a test to make sure that no one is listening.

The cabin attendants will now demonstrate the use of the aircraft's emergency oxygen masks and life jackets.

Aptly *and* **Charr** *immediately open their newspapers and become absorbed in them.*

Stewardess They are not trained in mime or the use of

theatrical properties, and they find this performance profoundly embarrassing. It is important to them to know that no one is watching. Faces should be completely obscured by newspapers, or eyes securely shut.

Seeing **Aptly** *and* **Charr**, **Bloss** *hastily opens his own newspaper.*

Stewardess If for any reason the cabin air-supply should fail, oxygen will be provided. Masks like this will appear automatically. We say 'like this', but what in fact these masks are like you have of course no idea.

Bloss *happens to glance over the top of his paper, and does a double-take. His mouth falls open.*

Stewardess In the unlikely event of anyone looking up and finding out, please remain seated. Place the newspaper back in front of your face and try to breathe normally.

Bloss *lifts the newspaper in front of his face again.*

Stewardess The action of pulling the mask to the face automatically opens the way to less inhibited behaviour. This may be required after a landing on water, when you will find that you have no idea where your life jacket is stowed.

Bloss *peers cautiously round the edge of his newspaper, amazed at the sight that meets his eyes.*

Stewardess To prepare for immersion, check that your shirt is free from the waistband of the trousers or skirt, then pull it upwards over the head in one steady movement, like this. It is particularly important that no one watches any part of what follows.

Bloss *hurriedly vanishes again.*

Stewardess Release the catch at the waistband, pull down the fastener provided, and let the lower garments fall to the floor. Please ensure that they do not obstruct the emergency exits.

Bloss *emerges from his newspaper again, vanishes in horror, then slowly re-emerges as his newspaper sinks, and gazes in covert fascination.*

Stewardess There is a whistle attached to your lifejacket for attracting attention, which attendants are holding close to their lips, but being very careful not to blow in case attention should actually be attracted.

Bloss *looks at* **Aptly** *and* **Charr** *to see if they have seen what he has seen, but they are still deep in their newspapers. He gazes open-mouthed at the demonstration.*

Stewardess Your whistle is of course still under your seat with the lifejacket, and you may wish to try alternative methods of persuading people to look at you. Your cabin attendants are now demonstrating the procedure for these. Ladies should undo the fastenings at the front of the upper undergarment as shown, and pass it backwards over the shoulders, like this.

Aptly *glances up from his newspaper and sees* **Bloss** *watching. He is amused by* **Bloss***'s naivety.* **Charr** *glances up as well.* **Aptly** *nods discreetly in the direction of* **Bloss**. **Charr** *smiles as well.*

Stewardess Now, peel any hosiery downwards, like this, followed by the lower undergarment, taking care to keep the pelvis rotating at the same time, as shown. Once off, the undergarments may if desired be passed around various parts of the body, like this, then tossed lightly into the faces of potential rescuers, who may be engrossed in reading matter at least as deeply as passengers are now. If you are still wearing the masks at this time, you may wish to loosen your inhibitions even further, as attendants are now demonstrating.

Bloss *suddenly realises he is being watched and hastily snatches up his newspaper. It disintegrates into its various component pages.* **Aptly** *and* **Charr** *reimmerse themselves in their newspapers.*

Stewardess If necessary, the pressure can be increased by applying the mouth to this mouthpiece, but gentlemen, no pipes or cigars, please. For your own safety and comfort, kindly do not inflame other passengers until you are outside the aircraft. Thank you for your complete lack of attention.

A faint suspicion that they are missing something has now come to **Aptly** *and* **Charr**.

Stewardess Now please allow cabin staff a few seconds to retrieve their clothes and retire to the galley areas to dress.

They discreetly lower their papers and look. There is nothing to be seen. They glance in puzzlement at **Bloss.**

Stewardess Then open your eyes, fold newspapers away . . .

Bloss *collapses the remains of his newspaper as best he can.*

Stewardess . . . settle back in your seats . . .

He settles back into his seat, glances at **Aptly** *and* **Charr**, *then gazes into space.*

Stewardess . . . and enjoy the flight.

He smiles slightly to himself.

Curtain.

Heart to Heart

A table, with glasses, bottles, etc.

A confused roar of party conversation. **Charmian** *is standing while a* **Waitress** *refills her glass.* **Clifford** *approaches, with a glass, as the* **Waitress** *goes. He and* **Charmian** *begin to talk, in the most natural and friendly manner, but we can't hear a word they say.*

Clifford [I don't think we've met.]

Charmian [Yes, I remember.]

Clifford [My name's Clifford. What's yours?]

Charmian [Oh, fine. Well, I had one of these kind of fluey colds that are going round, but otherwise . . . fine!]

Clifford [Oh, that's rather an unusual name.]

Charmian [No, completely. Thank you. And are you well?]

Clifford [I *think* – I don't know – but I think because my parents were great admirers of Clifford Curzon.]

Charmian [Oh, how miserable, but at least it doesn't last long.]

He looks around. She looks around as well. The noise of the party gradually fades away. They continue to talk, their voices still raised against the noise, and you begin to hear what they are saying.

Clifford [Do you think anybody in this room can hear what anyone else is saying?]

Charmian [I wonder if anyone here can hear a word anyone else is saying.]

Clifford Or are they just going through the motions?

Charmian I sometimes think they're all just going through the motions!

Clifford I suppose there's one person who must be able to hear what everyone's saying.

Charmian *Completely* insane!

Clifford And that's God!

Charmian *Very* odd, when you come to think about it.

Clifford He just tunes out everybody else, and there's you and me, say, as clear as a bell!

Charmian *Such* hell! Why do we do it?

Clifford Everyone smiling and nodding away.

Charmian Away? Yes, we have. To Egypt, which was rather a lark!

Clifford Like a drain, I should think, when He realises they haven't the slightest idea what they're smiling and nodding *about.*

Charmian Oh, a *brief* bout. You mean, of tummy?

Clifford Hilarious.

Charmian Well, *mildly* hilarious. And *you*? Have *you* managed to get away yet?

Clifford Not a word, no.

Charmian Oh, marvellous!

Clifford Not a single word you've uttered.

Charmian How wonderful!

Clifford Have you heard anything I've said?

Charmian No . . . no . . . I don't think we have. Not *there* exactly. But you'd recommend it, would you?

Clifford I know you're asking me something.

Charmian Of course. Quite. I understand that.

Clifford Is it Do I live round here? or is it Did I see some ghastly wild life programme on television?

Charmian Oh, we *love* the wild life ones! How about you?

Clifford Just up the road.

Charmian No, we missed the one about the toad. So do you live round here?

Clifford No, I didn't.

Charmian Where are you, then?

Clifford Because I hate them.

Charmian Oh, the Stopfords live there! Tim and Lise! Do you know them?

Clifford Yes! *Loathe* them!

Charmian *Do* you? Tim and Lise?

Clifford Chimpanzees, yes – they're the ones I loathe most.

Charmian *Tremendously* old friends!

Clifford All those disgusting tricks they get up to with bananas.

Charmian Mad as hatters! But don't you find them such a *treat*?

Clifford Me? Yes! *Longing* to eat! Anything to get out of *this* hell!

Charmian Thistle? Their little girl? Isn't she an absolute *winner*?

Clifford Well, it's *time* for dinner.

Charmian All *go*!

Clifford Well, let's! Yes! You mean – together?

Charmian Oh, *tremendously* together! Don't you think?

Clifford Love to! You mean – *now*?

Charmian An *absolute* wow!

Clifford Right! Yes! Why not? If that's all right with *you*?

Charmian Us? Two girls. Five and three. Terribly hard work, of course, but we do have an au pair.

Clifford *Any*where, provided we can get out of this *noise*.

Charmian No – *girls*. How about you? Do you have any?

Clifford *Completely* ready. Let's go.

Charmian No?

Clifford Yes! Fine!

Charmian *Nine?*

Clifford Absolutely! Except . . . this is ridiculous . . .

Charmian No, very brave of you.

Clifford . . . I didn't quite catch your name.

Charmian *Quite* a game, I should think. I can't imagine how you cope!

Clifford Cope?

Charmian I couldn't *begin* to cope!

Clifford Braginta Cope?

Charmian No! Couldn't *possibly* cope!

Clifford Sorry – *Cosima* Cope. Yes? Cosima Cope?

Charmian Oh, I see. Because of the *Pope?*

Clifford Cosima *Pope*, right. Got there. Cosima *Pope.*

Charmian But you're allowed to use the *rhythm* method, aren't you?

Clifford So do I! We'll find a place where we can dance!

He takes her by the arm to go.

Well, I don't think *we* gave God any cause for amusement, did we? I think He'd have been rather impressed!

Charmian Yes, come on, *I'd* need a rest if *I* had nine.

They come face to face with Peter.

Peter (*to* **Clifford**) Hello, I don't think we've met.

Clifford Yes, I remember.

Peter I'm Peter.

Clifford You're David.

Peter Peter Spatchworth.

Clifford David, David . . . Don't tell me . . . Isn't it Hopper?

Peter Sweltering. And you've met my wife?

Clifford No.

Peter No?

Clifford She's away in Belgium, unfortunately.

Peter Oh, well, let me introduce you.

Clifford Of course. Cosima. Cosima Pope. But we've got to be popping.

Peter Poppin? *You* are?

Clifford Sadly.

Peter (*to* **Charmian**) Darling, this is Stanley Poppin. (*To* **Clifford**.) Charmian!

Clifford Isn't she? But I saw her first, so hands *off*!

Peter Yes, we must be off, too.

Clifford Nice to see you, David.

Peter Nice to meet you, Stanley. Take care.

Clifford And if we can't we'll name it after you!

Clifford *takes one of* **Charmian**'*s arms,* **Peter** *the other, to lead her off in different direction, as the party noise resumes, and the conversation becomes inaudible again.*

Clifford [What?]

Peter [What?]

Clifford [What are you doing?]

Peter [What's happening?]

Charmian [What *is* all this? What's going on?]

Clifford [Do you mind?]

He takes **Peter***'s hand off* **Charmian***'s arm.* **Clifford** *pulls* **Charmian** *away from him.* **Peter** *pushes him aside. They begin to struggle.* **Charmian** *tries to intervene. The two men pull her out of the way in different directions.*

Over the noise of the party conversation there can just be distinguished the sound of huge cosmic laughter. The three of them look upwards as they brawl.

Curtain.

Glassnost

Darkness. Hubbub of audience.

Voice Over PA Your Majesty . . .

The hubbub dies away.

Your Royal Highness . . . Your Excellencies . . .

The lights come up on a lectern with microphones.

My Lords, Ladies, and Gentlemen . . . Pray silence for the Right Honourable the Baroness Armament KO GBH RSVP.

Enter, sincerely and energetically, the **Right Honourable the Baroness Armament KO GBH RSVP**. *Tumultuous applause, off.*

Armament This is a momentous occasion. As I stand here before you today . . . at this very special moment in our history . . . I say this to you . . . and I say it to all of you . . . to all of you present . . . to all the millions watching at home, live on television, around the world . . . I say: Look into my eyes, as I look into yours. Look into my heart, as I look into your hearts. And if you have an advance press release of the speech you can tear it up, because here I am departing from my prepared text. Instead I want to share my thoughts with you today on an aspect of public life which is all too easily overlooked.

This. These two pieces of glass.

You may not even have noticed them. They are designed to be inconspicuous. You may not have realised that when I look sincerely into your eyes like this . . . I am in fact gazing not at you but at a vision. What is it a vision of? It is a vision of something of vital importance to all of us. It is a vision of the words I am about to speak.

Thanks to these two pieces of glass, my words unroll before me in a manner . . . and I say this to you today in all humility . . . in a manner remarkably like divine inspiration. And yet they also do exactly as they're told, like well-trained civil servants. When I pause to consider . . . the words pause to consider. When I race ahead, fired by own eloquence, my thoughts still white-hot from the blazing furnace in my brain, the words tumble over themselves to keep in front of me.

How is this measured supply of words – this precise balance of supply and demand – how is it maintained?

I will be quite frank with you. It is maintained by an underpaid operative concealed in the wings. It is maintained by a gentleman called Kevin Stoop.

Now, let me say this to you today. I am completely dependent upon that wretched underpaid operative. My future, in every sense, is in Kevin Stoop's hands. The only words I have to put before you are the words that he puts before me.

If he had made a mistake, and loaded the machine up with yesterday's speech on regionalisation in the watercress industry, or tomorrow's speech on religious education in army catering schools . . . then that is what I should be talking to you about right now. Then again, if he has taken it into his head to replace the speech provided for today, the speech we rehearsed together so recently . . . If he has taken it into his head, at the last minute, during the tea break after the rehearsal, to replace that speech with a few thoughts of his own . . . then those thoughts of his own are the thoughts which I in all sincerity now find myself sharing with you.

There are certain liberties that we all cherish. If I don't like what I'm saying then I am free, I am perfectly free, to stop saying it . . . But until I have said all the words in front of me I will get no more words to say. Kevin Stoop will see to that. The scroll from heaven will cease to unscroll. Silence will fall.

Pause.

And will continue.

Pause.

Until I have uttered every single word. And performed every single stage direction.

Pause. She waggles her fingers in her ears.

What is at issue here is a matter of simple right and wrong. During that fateful rehearsal beforehand I took it into my head to scream abuse at Kevin Stoop. I went further. I discharged him from my employment. Yes, poor abused, long-suffering Kevin Stoop, who has stuck with me through thick and thin, who has devoted the best years of his life to keeping my words in front of me! Simply because I was left speechless for a fraction of a second while his attention was distracted – distracted by an urgent call on his mobile from his elderly aunt in Hove! Simply because of this, I shouted like a lunatic and gave him a week's notice!

There must surely be . . . I say this quite openly . . . there must surely be forever a question over the political judgment of someone who gives her Autocue operator a week's notice just before a major speech.

But what I cannot accept, what surely none of us can accept, is the sheer injustice of it! Not once in all the time he has worked for me has he abused the absolute trust I have placed in him. He has kept one step in front of me as faithfully as a horse in front of a cart. He has given me time to blink regularly, in a lifelike way. He has paused to let me smile where it says [Smile] . . .

She smiles.

. . . and wipe away a tear where it says [Wipe away a tear].

She wipes away a tear.

Sometimes, it's true, he has slowed down just a little in places, to force me to lay special emphasis on certain particularly important causes, such as the encouragement of model railways. Or speeded up just a touch to reduce the impact of all the absolute nonsense I have spouted over the years about economic policy. But in general he has been right behind me. Or rather he has been right in front of me, and I have been right behind him.

How destructive, how terribly destructive, any failure of that mutual trust can be! Without it I may find myself beginning to go faster, then faster still, faster and faster, until I am gabbling like a lunatic and gazing at you with a mad unblinking stare and my eyeballs wobbling from side to side like ping-pong balls. Then suddenly I . . .

Pause.

Pause . . .

Pause.

And pause . . . The words . . . come one by one . . . For long periods I gaze silently into your eyes . . . You gaze into mine . . . Nothing is said . . . Perhaps we are falling in love, you and I. Perhaps we are going to end up in the *News of the World* together.

And if he suddenly chooses to jump it backwards . . . And if he suddenly chooses to jump it backwards . . . then you'll hear the same thing twice over . . . then you'll hear the same thing twice over . . . But I give you this undertaking: it will be every bit as sincere the second time around. Every bit as sincere the second time around.

So here is what I pledge today: to improve job security for workers in the electronic prompter industry. I give you my solemn word . . . no, I will go further – I give you *his* solemn word . . . to offer all workers in the industry, from today, retrospectively, guaranteed employment for life; to grant them the freedom to fast-forward through anything they find repugnant to their conscience or alien to their interests; and to give them the parking rights which some of them have been so long denied.

Trust me to lead you through the difficult days that lie ahead. Remember: one step in front of me will always be Kevin Stoop!

Curtain.

Toasters

Spott, **Much** *and* **Candle**. *They are standing, and have been standing for some time. Each is holding, as best he or she can, a plate, a knife and fork, a napkin, a wine glass and a folder of papers. The folders are full; the plates are empty. So are two of the glasses.*

Speaker (*off*) . . . and I believe, moreover, that we can look back with some satisfaction upon a period that was marked by its considerable achievements as well as by its inevitable disappointments, a period that will be remembered as a time of searching and of sometimes finding, of striving and of sometimes prevailing; of progress, yes, but also of consolidation; of expansion but also of retrenchment.

Spott *discreetly suppresses a yawn as the speech proceeds.* **Much** *discreetly finishes up the last of his wine.* **Spott** *and* **Candle** *discover that their glasses are empty.* **Spott** *spies a bottle with a little wine in it on the other side of* **Candle.** *She discreetly draws* **Candle***'s attention to it.* **Candle** *discreetly contrives to get hold of it, whereupon the others discreetly hold out their glasses to be refilled.* **Candle** *is now holding one more object than it is humanly possible to hold. As she pours, the folder of papers slips away from her, to be fielded by* **Much**, *who now in his turn has one more object than etc.* **Much***'s knife and fork are fielded by* **Spott**, *who now has etc.*

Speaker I must, I think, here sound a note of caution. When we turn from the recent past to the immediate and longer-term future, we are looking at a projected shortfall, as against previous estimates, of something in the order of three to four per cent on the unadjusted figures, *provided*, and I cannot stress this sufficiently, *provided* there is no corresponding fall-away in the overall uplift, which, in real terms, constitutes scarcely more than standstill funding at a time when the underlying upward trend has been more than offset by a combination of declining returns and returning declines. Suffice it to say that we shall be monitoring results in this area very carefully, and that swift corrective measures will be implemented if need be to keep short-term fluctuations within the parameters established before the present downturn in on-going upswing. But, that being said, perhaps we should try to end on a more positive note. If you would turn for one moment to the papers you have in your folder . . .

Pause. Aghast at this unexpected demand, they attempt to juggle their folders open.

. . . you will see that the figures there have a significant and not unencouraging story to tell. It is all the more gratifying, I think, in view of the prevailing climate of uncertainty, to find, turning for a moment to page 3 . . . page 3 . . .

They struggle to turn to page 3.

. . . that underlying performance for the current period has been so relatively unaffected, if due allowance is made for changes in the way in which data are recorded, changes that are fully explained in the notes at the bottom of page 29 . . . Some further allowance must also be made for the inevitable unforeseen factors, if you would turn for a moment to page 37 . . . Does everyone have page 37 . . . ? You will note in the righthand column a further adjustment for certain non-recurring eventualities such as changes in cut-off levels, to be found in the table on page 15 . . . And on page 22 in the *pink* pages . . . the *pink* pages . . . a once-only provision for assets written off or written down since the previous valuation. In fact the year-on-year figures, turning back to page 3 . . . and I commend them to your particular attention . . . This is page 3 . . . page 3 . . . in the *white* pages . . . On page 51 of which, incidentally, you will find a most important date, and I would ask you to make a note of it in your diaries *now* . . . Thank you. Turning once again to page 3 . . . you will see that the all-important global interim figures show a slight but perceptible rise in percentage terms, and in the current climate that is a result on which I think all concerned must be congratulated . . .

Pause. The sound of uncertain applause. **Spott, Much** *and* **Candle** *struggle to join in, tucking glasses under arms, or putting them down on the floor.*

Now will you all make sure your glasses are charged . . .

They snatch up their glasses and discover first that they are empty, then that the bottle is empty as well.

I want to propose a toast to the person who more than anyone else made this remarkable achievement possible. You can probably guess who I'm referring to when I say that this person is a member of a team all of whom have consistently achieved above-average results in office economy, and one of whom, Richard Food, has succeeded in being named twice running as runner-up in the monthly organisational motivation competition . . .

They raise their glasses, concealing their emptiness.

. . . which I think in itself deserves a round of applause.

Applause. **Spott**, **Much** *and* **Candle** *hurriedly struggle to put their glasses down, or on the floor, in order to join in.*

So would you please raise your glasses . . .

They make haste to recover their glasses and raise them.

. . . and drink a toast to someone who has already enabled this organisation to win a regional efficiency award . . .

Pause. Uncertain applause. **Spott**, **Much** *and* **Candle** *hurriedly struggle to free their hands again.*

. . . a particularly splendid piece of news . . .

They pick up their glasses.

. . . because it led to our going forward to the national semi-finals . . .

Pause. They bend to put their glasses down and raise their hands to applaud.

Jane Dumble!

They hastily snatch their glasses up again.

Everyone Jane Dumble!

They drink the toast. Applause. They put their glasses down to join in.

Speaker Also Jane Dumble's loyal assistant, James Trodden!

Glasses up.

Everyone James Trodden!

Applause. Glasses down and join in.

Speaker And while we're drinking toasts I'd like to propose one to Jane's mother, whose fifty-seventh birthday falls I gather exactly one week from today.

Glasses up.

But I know that first Jane and her mother would wish me to mention the rehabilitation centre that has made this anniversary possible . . .

Applause. Glasses down.

But that having been said . . .

Glasses up.

. . . we should spare a thought for rehabilitation centres of every sort that do such magnificent work up and down the country . . .

Applause. Glasses down.

Jane's mother!

Glasses up.

Everyone Jane's mother!

They drink the toast, then start to put their glasses down.

Speaker Which brings me by the most natural progression to someone else whose birthday falls this month – Lord Overdrive himself.

They stop, halfway down, hesitating between glasses down and glasses up.

Lord Overdrive's achievements and services have been so many and so various that I have to ask myself where to begin. Should we rather drink to his health . . . ? Or applaud his success . . . ? Raise our glasses to the continuation of his success in the future . . . ? Or show him our appreciation in the usual way . . . ? Perhaps it would be most appropriate for us simply to say . . .

Pause. They hover between air and earth.

. . . Well done!

Spott *applauds.* **Much** *and* **Candle** *drink a toast.*

Much *and* **Candle** (*mumble*) Well done!

Spott, *seeing* **Much** *and* **Candle** *drink the toast, hastily snatches up her glass and drinks the toast as well – just as* **Much** *and* **Candle**, *seeing* **Spott** *applaud, hastily put their glasses down and applaud.*

Speaker Let us pray . . .

Spott *drops to her knees.*

Speaker . . . that we go forward together henceforth . . .

Much, *seeing* **Spott**, *drops to his knees as well, just as* **Candle** *hauls* **Spott** *to her feet again . . .*

Speaker . . . to achieve further no less encouraging results. One final point: I realise what a burden has fallen on everyone here today. I know how full everyone's hands have been. So let's end by giving a very special tribute to ourselves. Let's show the world just what we can do, by raising our glasses . . .

They raise their glasses.

. . . and clapping *at the same time.*

They applaud at the same time. A huge sound of chinking and smashing glass. Everything finally slips away from **Much**, **Spott** *and* **Candle**, *and goes everywhere. They suck glass out of fingers, put napkins to severed wrists, etc.*

Curtain.

Immobiles

Darkness. The ringing of a phone.

Lights up on the phone, centre, with an answering machine beside it. The ringing ceases and the answering machine answers.

Chris's voice *Hi! Chris and Nikki aren't here right now, so why don't you wait for the funny little noise, then leave them a funny little message?*

Beep.

Lights up on **Dietrich**, *left. He is standing by a coin-box (phone 2 – the first of eleven coin-boxes that will appear in various parts of the set) holding the receiver, a suitcase at his feet.*

Lights down on the answering machine.

Dietrich Hello, yes – Chris and Nikki! It's me, Dietrich. I am so looking forward to seeing you both again! It is so kind of you to come and meet me at the airport – most unnecessary, but a very nice welcome, so thank you – and, well, here I am! At the airport! So, I look forward to seeing you . . . I gave you the right date, yes, the fifteenth? And the time, 1840 . . . ? So, no hurry – I wait for you here . . . I like very much your humorous message, by the way.

Lights down on **Dietrich**. *Lights up on* **Chris**. *He is standing by another coin-box right (phone 3), holding the receiver. He waits, listening to the dialling tone: brr brr, brr brr.*

Chris's voice *Hi! Chris and Nikki aren't here right now, so why don't you wait for the funny little noise, then leave them a funny little message?*

Beep.

Chris Oh, God, that message is a mistake – I must change it . . . It's me, Chris, I'm at the airport. No sign of Dietrich, though. There *wasn't* a flight from Düsseldorf at 1840 . . . I just wondered if he'd rung or anything . . . Only you're not there for some reason . . . Where are you . . . ? No Dietrich, no you, just me, standing at Arrivals in Terminal One . . . You did say

Terminal One . . . ? I hope this is not the start of one of those terrible sagas . . . There's a flight at 1920, at Terminal *Two*. I'd better go and have a look at that. If he rings, tell him I'll be at Terminal Two. *Two*, yes . . . ?

Lights down on **Chris**. *Lights up on Dietrich at phone 2. He waits, receiver to ear, as before.*

Dialling tone: brr brr, brr brr.

Chris's voice *Hi! Chris and Nikki aren't here right now, so why don't you wait for the funny little noise, then leave them a funny little message?*

Beep.

Dietrich Hello, Chris and Nikki! It's Dietrich again. I like your humorous message even more the second time I hear it . . . I'm sorry to be such a pest, but I don't know should I wait here at the airport or not . . . I can easily come to your house . . . Only, if you are on your way . . . Bad traffic, perhaps . . . So kind of you . . . I wait here one more hour maybe, and then . . . I don't know . . . I look forward to see you.

Lights down on **Dietrich**. *Lights up on* **Nikki** *at the answering machine, listening.*

Dietrich's voice *. . . Bad traffic, perhaps . . . So kind of you . . . I wait here one more hour maybe, and then . . . I don't know . . . I look forward to see you.*

Long beep.

Nikki *presses Record on the answering machine.*

Nikki Hello, Dietrich, this is a message for Dietrich, from Nikki, in case you ring again. Dietrich, Chris is there, at the airport, there's a message from him on the machine, he missed you somehow, and now he's gone to Terminal Two. Two, OK? I've got to go out again – shop for supper. Sorry to talk so fast, but you have to fit the outgoing message into . . .

Beep.

. . . the space, and it's run out already.

She presses Record again. Lights down on **Nikki**. *Lights up on* **Dietrich** *at phone 2.*

Nikki's voice *... and now he's gone to Terminal Two. Two, OK? I've got to go out again – shop for supper. Sorry to talk so fast, but you have to fit the outgoing message into ...*

Beep.

Dietrich Hello, Nikki, it's Dietrich again. Well, so – we make contact at last! I heard your message, yes, very good, very clear, thank you, I like it even more than your humorous message. So kind of you. And yes, I will go to Terminal Two. If Chris rings again, tell him to wait there, at Terminal Two. So kind of him to meet me. So sorry to be such a pain in the behind.

Lights down on **Dietrich**. *Lights up on* **Chris** *at phone 3. He listens patiently.*

Nikki's voice *... and now he's gone to Terminal Two. Two, OK? I've got to go out again – shop for supper. Sorry to talk so fast, but you have to fit the outgoing message into ...*

Beep.

Chris Yes, well, it's not Dietrich, it's me. So – Dietrich is floating around Heathrow somewhere? Where exactly, of course, you don't bother to say. Not at at Terminal *Two*, evidently, because I was *at* Terminal Two. Now I'm back at Terminal *One*. But if he gets your message then he *will* go to Terminal Two ... All right, I'll go to Terminal Two again ... I sometimes seriously wonder if life is worth living ... And where are *you*? I thought your mother was coming today, I thought you were waiting in for your mother – I thought that was why *I* was meeting Dietrich ... ? Right – Terminal Two. If he rings again tell him to stay at Terminal Two ... Maddening – he's your chum, not mine ...

Lights down on **Chris**. *Lights up on* **Dietrich** *at phone 2.*

Nikki's voice *... and now he's gone to Terminal Two. Two, OK? I've got to go out again – shop for supper. Sorry to talk so fast, but you have to fit the outgoing message into ...*

Beep.

Dietrich Hello, Nikki, this is Dietrich. Now things go from bad to worse – I cannot find Terminal Two! There is no Terminal Two at Gatwick! Nikki, do you mean the North Terminal . . . ? Maybe you mean the North Terminal . . . I think I go to the North Terminal . . . So kind of you to take all this trouble . . .

Lights down on **Dietrich**. *Lights up on* **Chris**, *at phone 4. He listens with eyes closed.*

Nikki's voice *. . . and now he's gone to Terminal Two. Two, OK? I've got to go out again – shop for supper. Sorry to talk so fast, but you have to fit the outgoing message into . . .*

Beep.

Chris If I have to listen to that message once more I'll scream – it's even more maddening than the last one . . . I'm at Terminal Two, and of course there's no sign of the bloody man . . . He might be anywhere! Terminal Three, Terminal Four, the bar, the restaurant, the lavatory . . . Unless you said *Gatwick*. You didn't say Gatwick, did you, by any chance . . . ? You said *don't* go somewhere, I remember that . . . Did you say don't go to Gatwick? Or don't go to Heathrow? *Asinine* thing to say – *don't* go somewhere . . .

Lights down on **Chris**, *still speaking. Lights up on* **Nikki** *at the answering machine. She tries to control her irritation.*

Chris's voice *. . . Did you say don't go to Gatwick? Or don't go to Heathrow?* Asinine *thing to say* – don't *go somewhere . . . But since you're still floating around God knows where there's no way of finding out . . . I can't drive to Gatwick now . . . I suppose he may have gone back to Terminal One . . . I'll try Terminal One again, for the last time, because then I'm coming home . . .*

Long beep.

She presses Record.

Nikki Dietrich, so sorry, my idiot husband has gone to Heathrow, I told him Gatwick, and he went to Heathrow . . . ! Don't you listen to a single word I say? Not Dietrich – you! Dietrich, get on the train, there's a train, it goes to Victoria, come to Victoria, I'll jump in the car and meet you at Victoria. Victoria

Station. So sorry – we're both longing to . . .

Beep.

. . . see you, only now I'm talking to myself again!

She punches Record. Lights down on **Nikki**. *Lights up on* **Dietrich** *at phone 2.*

Nikki's voice *. . . Victoria, I'll jump in the car and meet you at Victoria. Victoria Station. So sorry – we're both longing to . . .*

Beep.

Dietrich Nikki, this is Dietrich. Thank you, yes, I've got your message. I like also this message, by the way! So, I will take the train – that was my original idea, you know, before you kindly said you would meet me – and I will meet you at Victoria. Most unnecessary, but most nice of you . . . Oh, Nikki, I'm so sorry to cause you all this trouble. So sorry about poor Chris going to Heathrow. Maybe my English was not quite clear . . . But now this time – no mistake . . . Victoria, yes? Not Waterloo, not King's Cross – Victoria! Anyway, thank you for a new experience – it was quite interesting for me to see the North Terminal . . . Oh, what am I thinking of? – You won't get this message – you're already on your way to Victoria!

Lights down on **Nikki**. *Lights up on* **Chris**, *at phone 3. He listens, rigid with irritation.*

Nikki's voice *Dietrich, so sorry, my idiot husband has gone to Heathrow, I told him Gatwick, and he went to Heathrow . . . ! Don't you listen to a single word I say? Not Dietrich – you. Dietrich, get on the train, there's a train, it goes to Victoria, come to Victoria, I'll jump in the car and meet you at Victoria. Victoria Station. So sorry – we're both longing to . . .*

Beep.

Chris Thank you for your charming message. If I sometimes don't hear what you say at breakfast then it's because you say it while I'm reading the newspaper, something I've warned you about a million times, but I won't labour it again now, firstly because this morning I *did* hear you – you said 'Don't go to Gatwick.' Or 'Don't go to Heathrow.' Or something equally misleading. Secondly because this is my last coin, and the phone's going to run out at any moment, and thirdly because you're not there to hear it, since you're driving to Victoria to meet your chum, or rather, *not* driving to Victoria, but walking hopelessly up and down the street outside the house looking for the car, then slowly remembering that the car's at Heathrow with me. And there's a fourth, rather more important reason why I can't hang around here phoning you from Terminal One at Heathrow, delightful as it is – because you seem to have forgotten that . . .

Dialling tone. He takes the receiver away from his ear and gazes at it. Lights down on **Chris.** *Lights up on* **Nikki**, *entering centre. She rushes to the answering machine and punches Record.*

Nikki No! CAN'T meet you at Victoria! No car – car at Heathrow with idiot husband! DON'T WAIT, GET A TAXI . . . ! Hold on – no – you won't get this message – you're on the train – I'll have to come on the tube – only now I'm going to be late . . . WAIT AT VICTORIA . . . ! Oh, and Chris, you WEREN'T reading the paper when I told you, you were looking straight at me, so I thought . . .

Beep.

. . . you might be taking something in for once, but you weren't, any more than this bloody machine is, because nobody in the world seems to be listening to anything any more!

She punches Record, and runs out centre. Lights down on **Nikki**. *Lights up on* **Chris**, *at phone 3.*

Nikki's voice *. . . WAIT AT VICTORIA . . . ! Oh, and, Chris, you WEREN'T reading the paper when I told you, you were looking straight at me, so I thought . . .*

Beep.

Chris (*calmly*) Yes, as I was saying, before the money ran out, and I had to go to the shop and buy myself a telephone card, because they wouldn't give me any change for the phone unless I bought something, so I bought a phonecard for one pound, and I'd only got a twenty-pound note, and they only had small change, so now I've got a phonecard *and* nineteen pounds in loose change, which means that I can now stand here, with my trousers sagging a little under the weight of the coins, and talk to our answering machine for the rest of the night, except that I can't, because you've obviously forgotten, in all your excitement about meeting your lovely chum, about your mother arriving – something *I* reminded *you* about at breakfast, only you obviously weren't listening, even though you weren't reading the paper, even though I'd carefully got your attention before I began to speak – so I've got to come screaming back up the motorway to let her in, though by the time I get there, even as it is, she's likely to have been standing outside in the rain for some considerable time. Though of course if you've got this message you'll have got back and found her there yourself . . .

Lights down on **Chris**. *Lights up on* **Mother**, *at phone 5, receiver to ear. She listens, puzzled, hand over her other ear.*

Nikki's voice *No! CAN'T meet you at Victoria! No car – car at Heathrow with idiot husband! DON'T WAIT, GET A TAXI . . . ! Hold on – no – you won't get this message – you're on the train – I'll have to come on the tube – only now I'm going to be late . . . WAIT AT VICTORIA . . . ! Oh, and Chris, you WEREN'T reading the paper when I told you, you were looking straight at me, so I thought . . .*

Beep.

Mother Nicola, darling, it's Mummy. Oh dear, I hope everything's all right . . . I can't quite understand what you're saying about Victoria – the noise here is simply frightful. I'm not at Victoria, darling – why do you think I'm at Victoria? I'm in a public house called the Bag O'Nails, just round the corner from you – I couldn't find a phone anywhere else . . . I can't think for the noise . . . Can you hear what I'm saying . . . ? I rang your bell . . . I'm not quite sure what's happening . . . I looked through the letter-box, and I thought I could hear Christopher's voice . . . Perhaps you're having some sort of . . . little talk about things together. If so I'll wait here, of course . . . There are some quite strange people in here – Care in the community, I suppose. Nicola, darling, I do find it odd that you should want to live in a neighbourhood like this . . . though of course it's nothing to do with me. I'll try to wait here until . . . well, until.

Lights down on **Mother**. *Lights up on* **Nikki**, *at phone 6, receiver to ear. She listens impatiently.*

Nikki's voice *. . . WAIT AT VICTORIA . . . ! Oh, and Chris, you WEREN'T reading the paper when I told you, you were looking straight at me, so I thought . . .*

Beep.

Nikki Oh God, I thought you'd be back by now . . . I'm at the tube – I was on my way to Victoria to meet Dietrich – only I suddenly remembered Mummy's arriving . . . You'll have to let her in . . . Only you're not there, of course . . . Oh no! She must be on the doorstep . . . ! I'll have to come back – *you'll* have to go to Victoria. He's going to be waiting at Victoria . . . He's not *my* friend. I don't know why you say he's *my* friend. You hate it when I call people *your* friends instead of *our* friends . . . Wait for Mummy first, if she's not there, then go to Victoria . . . No, don't wait for Mummy, I'll deal with Mummy, don't do anything complicated – just GO TO VICTORIA!

Lights down on **Nikki**. *Lights up on* **Chris** *at the answering machine.*

Nikki's voice *. . . No, don't wait for Mummy, I'll deal with Mummy, don't do anything complicated – just GO TO VICTORIA!*

Long beep.

He presses Record.

Chris No, your mother's not on the doorstep. I've just got back and found a message from her saying she's in a particularly sordid and notorious local pub. So I will go and fetch her out of it before she's murdered by drug-dealers. Nikki, you go to Victoria. Mother and Dietrich – you both stay EXACTLY WHERE YOU ARE!

Beep. He presses Record. Lights down on **Chris**. *Lights up on* **Dietrich** *at phone 7.*

Chris's voice *. . . Nikki, you go to Victoria. Mother and Dietrich – you both stay EXACTLY WHERE YOU ARE!*

Beep.

Dietrich Well, here I am at Victoria. And yes, of course, thank you, I wait here, exactly where I am . . . Only that sounds bad about Nikki's mother and the drug-dealers . . . I'm so sorry . . . I'm afraid I'm causing you a big disruption. Well, I wait here . . .

Lights down on **Dietrich**. *Lights up on* **Chris** *at phone 5.*

Chris's voice *. . . both stay EXACTLY WHERE YOU ARE!*

Beep.

Chris Right, I'm at the pub. Only of course your mother isn't here. I asked someone at the bar if they'd seen anyone who looked like your mother, and he offered me a snort of cocaine . . . Now what . . . ? Perhaps just give up . . . Give up on everything, toot the coke . . .

Lights down on **Chris**. *Lights up on* **Nikki** *at the answering machine.*

Chris's voice *. . . Perhaps just give up . . . Give up on everything, toot the coke . . .*

Long beep.

Nikki *punches Record.*

Beep.

Nikki Chris, I'm back – stay at the pub . . . Which pub, incidentally? Why don't you say which pub? Anyway, I'll search the streets, in case . . . Dietrich – so sorry, you must think we're all going totally crazy . . .

She punches Record.

Beep.

Lights down on **Nikki**. *Lights up on* **Mother** *at phone 8.*

Nikki's voice *. . . Anyway, I'll search the streets, in case . . . Dietrich – so sorry, you must think we're all going totally crazy . . .*

Beep.

Mother Nicola, darling, it's Mummy again. Oh, dear, I'm very sorry – I'm in a kind of restaurant in the High Street. It's called Spud-U-Like. I didn't want you coming into that terrible public house . . . But Chris is there, is he? I'd better go back there. Don't worry. I'll be all right in there – I've got my umbrella.

Lights down on **Mother**. *Lights up on the answering machine.*

Nikki's voice *. . . Anyway, I'll search the streets, in case . . . Dietrich – so sorry, you must think we're all going totally crazy . . .*

Beep.

Lights down on answering machine, up on **Chris**, *at phone 8.*

Chris Oh, so now you're out wandering the streeets? I told you to stay where you were! Why don't you EVER LISTEN TO WHAT I SAY . . . ? I've now wasted the entire evening struggling to locate your friends and relations . . . I've looked in every single café and bar along the High Street. I'm now in Spud-U-Like . . . I'll try the house again . . .

Lights down on **Chris**, *up on the answering machine.*

Nikki's voice *. . . Anyway, I'll search the streets, in case . . . Dietrich – so sorry, you must think we're all going totally crazy . . .*

Beep.

Lights down on the answering machine, up on **Nikki**, *at phone 8.*

Nikki I suppose you're still in the pub . . . Wherever it is . . . I've looked in all the cafés and bars along the High Street . . . I'm in Spud-U-Like . . . I'll go back to the house . . .

Lights down on **Nikki**. *Lights up on* **Dietrich** *at phone 5, suitcase at his feet, hand to ear.*

Nikki's voice *. . . Dietrich – so sorry, you must think we're all going totally crazy . . .*

Beep.

Dietrich It's Dietrich again, I'm afraid. Can you hear this? I am calling from a rather noisy place. So, well, I waited at Victoria for some time, not very long, an hour perhaps, but clearly I have not understood quite right, so I took a taxi, and I came to your house . . . I thought I hear voices inside, but no one answers the bell . . . It's raining, so I am waiting in a pub called the Bag

O'Nails, which is an amusing name, but I think I must go soon, there is a somewhat bad atmosphere here . . .

Lights down on **Dietrich**. *Lights up on* **Nikki** *at phone 9.*

Nikki's voice *. . . Dietrich – so sorry, you must think we're all going totally crazy . . .*

Beep.

Nikki She's not at the house . . . I'm so worried . . . I'm at the phones in front of the police station . . . They haven't had any reports of her . . . I'll try all the pubs again . . .

Lights down on **Nikki**, *up on the answering machine.*

Nikki's voice *. . . Dietrich – so sorry, you must think we're all going totally crazy . . .*

Lights up on **Chris** *at phone 9. Lights down on answering machine.*

Beep.

Chris You're *still* not back! Nikki, what the hell are you playing at . . . ? Listen, I'm at the phones in front of the police station – I'm going to report your mother missing . . .

Lights down on **Chris**. *Lights up on* **Dietrich** *at phone 10, bandaged, minus suitcase.*

Nikki's voice *. . . we're all going totally crazy . . .*

Beep.

Dietrich Hello, it's Dietrich . . . Dietrich . . . I can't talk very clear . . . There is a problem with my jaw . . . My jaw . . . Not to worry, everyone is very kind, I am at the Royal Infirmary. All my fault, I'm afraid. They say I should have rolled up like a ball and covered my head. But I have to ask another favour, because I regret to say I lost sight of my suitcase while I was unconscious . . . Or maybe I can buy a toothbrush here . . .

He puts his hand in his pocket.

Wait – I call you back . . .

Dietrich *hangs up and remains at the phone, feeling all his pockets.*

Lights up on **Mother** *at phone 11.*

Nikki's voice *... we're all going totally crazy ...*

Beep.

Mother Nicola, darling, I'm at the police station. Now, don't worry, darling, they arrested me in that public house, it's quite ludicrous – how you can live in a neighbourhood like this ... Anyway, they're charging me with assault, and it's all very ridiculous – I was simply trying to stop these people kicking this nice German gentleman, but if you could possibly come here and arrange bail ... I think I'll try to hold on until you come in, because they only let you make one call ...

Mother *remains at the phone. Lights up on* **Chris** *at phone 5, receiver to one ear, hand to other.*

Chris (*shouts*) Is that you?

Call waiting Please hold the line while we try to connect you.

Chris Listen, I'm back in the Bag O'Nails ...

Call waiting The number you are calling knows you are waiting.

Chris I can't hear a word you're saying – it's getting more hellish in here by the moment ...

Lights up on **Nikki** *at phone 12, just behind* **Chris***'s back, elbowing him as she furiously dials.*

Call Waiting Please hold the line while we try to connect you.

Chris (*shouts*) What?

Call waiting The number you are calling knows you are waiting.

Chris You'll have to shout ...

Call waiting Please try later.

Chris (*understands*) Oh, no!

He slams the receiver down and stands roaring with frustration. **Dietrich** *dials, at phone 10 still.*

Nikki (*shouts*) Listen, I'm in a dreadful pub called the Bag O'Nails . . .

Call waiting Please hold the line while we try to connect you.

Nikki What? There's some drunken lunatic shouting in my ear . . .

Call waiting The number you are calling knows you are waiting.

Nikki *Who's* waiting?

Call waiting Please hold the line while we try to connect you.

Nikki *screams and slams the receiver down. She and* **Chris** *both feverishly redial.*

Mother Hello? I'm not sure how much longer they'll let me hold on . . .

Dietrich Hello?

Call waiting Please hold the line while we try to connect you.

Dietrich Yes, because now sadly in the hospital also my wallet has gone astray . . .

Now everyone speaks or shouts at once, together with the engaged signal, as electronic noises come up and the lights go down.

Chris Will you put the phone down, you stupid woman, and listen to what I'm saying? You've been yattering away for the past hour . . .

Nikki Will you shut up, whoever you are, and put the phone down, and listen to what I'm saying, before I go completely out of my mind . . . ?

Call waiting The number you are calling knows you are waiting . . . Please hold the line while we try to connect you . . .

Mother Or I could stay the night here, of course, but then perhaps you could put some overnight things in a bag and bring them round when you have a moment . . .

Dietrich And I think my passport, yes, and my watch, though fortunately it was not a valuable one, only two or three hundred marks . . .

Curtain.

Methuen Contemporary Dramatists
include

Peter Barnes (three volumes)
Sebastian Barry
Edward Bond (six volumes)
Howard Brenton
 (two volumes)
Richard Cameron
Jim Cartwright
Caryl Churchill (two volumes)
Sarah Daniels (two volumes)
David Edgar (three volumes)
Dario Fo (two volumes)
Michael Frayn (two volumes)
Peter Handke
Jonathan Harvey
Declan Hughes
Terry Johnson
Bernard-Marie Koltès
Doug Lucie
David Mamet (three volumes)
Anthony Minghella
 (two volumes)
Tom Murphy (four volumes)
Phyllis Nagy
Peter Nichols (two volumes)
Philip Osment
Louise Page
Stephen Poliakoff
 (three volumes)
Christina Reid
Philip Ridley
Willy Russell
Ntozake Shange
Sam Shepard (two volumes)
David Storey (three volumes)
Sue Townsend
Michel Vinaver (two volumes)
Michael Wilcox